I AM MY BROTHER'S KEEPER

EXPLORING BIBLICAL BROTHERHOOD,
PURPOSE, AND UNBREAKABLE BONDS

TONY AUSTIN JR.

I AM MY BROTHER'S KEEPER

Exploring Biblical Brotherhood, Purpose, and Unbreakable Bonds

Author: Tony Austin Jr.

Copyright © 2025

All rights reserved. No part of this book may be reproduced or transmitted in any form or by any means, electronic or mechanical, including photocopying, recording, or by an information storage and retrieval system – except by a reviewer who may quote brief passages in a review to be printed in a magazine, newspaper, or on the Web – without permission in writing from the Author.

Edition: Paperback | Hardcover | eBook

Printed and bound in the United States of America.

DISCLAIMER

This book is intended for educational and informational purposes only. It does not constitute financial, investment, tax, or legal advice. Reading this book does not create a client–advisor relationship.

Every financial situation is unique. Before making any decisions, consult with qualified professionals who understand your personal circumstances and the applicable laws in your jurisdiction.

The examples, tools, and strategies shared are based on general knowledge and experience in the financial field. While efforts have been made to ensure accuracy, no results are guaranteed, and the author and publisher are not responsible for outcomes related to the application of this content.

ACKNOWLEDGEMENT

To the brothers who've walked beside me—this book wouldn't exist without your example, your encouragement, and your presence. Some of you led with wisdom. Others showed up with a word, a warning, or just a steady presence when I needed it most. Each of you, in your own way, reminded me what brotherhood really looks like.

To my father—thank you for the foundation you laid, for the moments you led by example, and for the ones where I learned what not to do. Both shaped me. Both taught me. Your journey helped carve mine, and I honor the man you were and the man you pushed me to become.

To my brother—I'm proud of the man of God you are daily becoming. Your walk reminds me that growth is ongoing, and godly strength is forged step by step.

To Apostle Carlos L. Malone Sr.—your apostolic covering, spiritual leadership, and godly example have shaped me more than words can capture. I'm honored to be under your mantle.

To the men of the Men's Ministry—you have been iron sharpening iron. From prayer circles to real conversations, you've shown that manhood and faith are not in conflict—they're forged together. Your walk inspires mine.
To the men whose names may never make a platform but who've made a difference in my life—you are seen. Brothers in Christ, mentors, teachers, friends—you've helped me carry weight I didn't always know I was holding.

Thank you for being keepers. For covering me when I couldn't see. For walking with me when I didn't have words. For showing me what it means to be a man of God in real time.

This book is for you, because before I could ever write about being my brother's keeper—I had to experience it.

And to the next generation of men—those still finding their voice, their calling, their footing—this is for you. May these pages strengthen your heart, stretch your faith, and stir up the keeper inside of you.

Thank you for being keepers. For covering me when I couldn't see. For walking with me when I didn't have words. For showing me what it means to be a man of God in real time.

This book is for you, because before I could ever write about being my brother's keeper—I had to experience it.

TABLE OF CONTENT

Forward	1
The Keeper's Challenge	3
Chapter 1: Shadows from Our Past	5
Chapter 2: The Unseen Bond	13
Chapter 3: Echoes of Brotherhood	19
Chapter 4: Guardian of Secrets	25
Chapter 5: Shared Paths, Divergent Journeys	33
Chapter 6: In the Mirror of Memory	45
Chapter 7: Unspoken Understandings	51
Chapter 8: Tangled Threads of Fate	57
Chapters 9: Two Halves of a Whole	65
Chapter 10: Silent Sacrifices	73
Chapter 11: Built to Lead: The Call of the Older Man	81
Chapter 12: Legacy of Love and Loss	89
About The Author	99

FORWARD

Brotherhood is a very traditional language used over the years to express the beloved bond between men, and even women in some contextual narratives. In Tony Austin's manuscript presentation, *I Am My Brother's Keeper*, he explores relative topics great for relational discourse and conversation. Knowing Tony as my spiritual son and Executive Pastor, I can say without fear of successful contradiction that this is a passionate heart matter for him. This book is not just his passion but his pursuit.

So many people have opined on the subject of men and mankind, but not many go into the depth of it with personal application and transparency. Some people write just to make a statement; Tony wrote this book to make a point and to parallel a relative connection and conversation that challenges other men to get engaged and involved.

This is a mission and a mandate, so read this book as such. Don't skip a page. Eat it all, and may the drumbeat of passion stir your soul and bring a conviction to your heart as a man that says, *I, too, am my brother's keeper.*

Congratulations, son. Job well done, and much success on the journey.

Apostle Carlos L. Malone Sr.
Apostolic Overseer: The Bethel Church Miami

THE KEEPER'S CHALLENGE

Every man reaches a moment when he looks around and sees that something sacred has been torn down. The walls that were supposed to protect—whether in our families, our churches, or our personal lives—are cracked, broken, or missing altogether. That moment demands a response.

For Nehemiah, that moment came when word reached him that the walls of Jerusalem were still in ruins. He wasn't a priest. He wasn't a warrior. But he was a man who cared enough to act. He mourned, he prayed, and then he moved. What followed wasn't just a construction project; it was a mission. And the moment he stepped into it, opposition showed up too.

Enemies mocked him. Doubts crept in. The people he led grew tired. But Nehemiah didn't flinch. He built with one hand and defended with the other. And through it all, he never stopped pointing the people back to their source of strength: *"Our God will fight for us"* (Nehemiah 4:20).

That same grit and spiritual focus is echoed in Jesus' words to Peter in Matthew 16:18: *"You are Peter, and on this rock I will build my church, and the gates of Hades will not overcome it."*

This wasn't just a promise; it was a charge. It was God declaring that His people would be builders. Men of foundation. Men of courage. Men who don't walk away from brokenness but walk straight into it purposefully.

That's what this book is about.

Being your brother's keeper means more than being a friend. It's about covering, protecting, stepping in when things fall apart, and standing up when others step back. It's not always convenient. It's not always clean. But it's always needed.

Maybe you've seen it firsthand—a struggling marriage, a fractured church, a brother walking away from the faith. It's easy to watch from a distance and say, "That's not my problem." But keepers don't think that way. Keepers get involved. They pray. They lead. They show up.

I once heard about a small church that was ready to close its doors. People had left. Money was tight. Hope was low. But a few men decided to fight for it. Not with big speeches or dramatic gestures, but with consistency. They fasted. They met. They cleaned the building. They knocked on doors. They became visible. And slowly, life returned. That's the power of presence. That's the keeper's role.

This introduction is your invitation. Before you go deeper into the stories that follow—stories of brothers, friends, protectors, and builders—I want you to reflect:

Where am I needed?
What's been broken on my watch?
Am I ready to do something about it?

Because the truth is simple: God still calls men to build. He still calls men to keep. And He still gives strength to those willing to say, "Yes."

Let's go.

CHAPTER 1

Shadows from Our Past

Something is haunting about shadows. They don't make noise. They don't leave fingerprints. But they follow us everywhere. You can't run from them. You can't outpace them. Shadows don't always mean evil, but they do remind us of what once was. And every man, whether he admits it or not, has some shadows trailing behind him.

Some are the result of what we did. Others stem from what we didn't do. And many are tied to the people we were supposed to protect but didn't. The decisions we made when we were angry. The words we never apologized for. The moments we looked away instead of leaning in. These moments create shadows—emotional echoes of responsibility avoided, pain caused, and chances missed.

From the very beginning of humanity's story, we're faced with this question: *Am I my brother's keeper?* (Genesis 4:9). That wasn't just a moment between Cain and God. That was a divine echo—a question that still demands an answer today.

The Echoes of Genesis

To understand the weight of that question, we've got to go back to the source. Genesis 4:1–16 (NKJV) gives us the first recorded act of brotherhood—and betrayal:

Now Adam knew Eve his wife, and she conceived and bore Cain, and said, "I have acquired a man from the Lord." Then she bore again, this time his brother Abel.

Now Abel was a keeper of sheep, but Cain was a tiller of the ground. And in the process of time, it came to pass that Cain brought an offering of the fruit of the ground to the Lord. Abel also brought of the firstborn of his flock and their fat. And the Lord respected Abel and his offering, but He did not respect Cain and his offering. And Cain was very angry, and his countenance fell.

So, the Lord said to Cain, "Why are you angry? And why has your countenance fallen? If you do well, will you not be accepted? And if you do not do well, sin lies at the door. And its desire is for you, but you should rule over it."

Now Cain talked with Abel his brother; and it came to pass, when they were in the field, that Cain rose up against Abel his brother and killed him.

Then the Lord said to Cain, "Where is Abel your brother?"

He said, "I do not know. Am I my brother's keeper?"

And He said, "What have you done? The voice of your brother's blood cries out to Me from the ground..."

Now pause right there. Cain didn't answer God with repentance. He responded with deflection. With attitude. With distance. And yet, God still engaged him. Because even in discipline, God doesn't disconnect.

This story is often labeled "the first murder." But it's more than that. It's the first example of one man refusing to take ownership of another. The first case where comparison, jealousy, and internal competition boil over into violence. This is the first record of a brother walking out of alignment with God's heart—and a consequence that would follow him for life.

What's so dangerous is that Cain's attitude didn't begin with murder; it started with resentment. With a bruised ego. With that inner voice that whispers, "Why him and not me?" (Genesis 4:5).

This is a question that men still wrestle with today—especially when someone else is celebrated and we feel overlooked.

God warned him: "Sin is crouching at the door... but you must rule over it" (Genesis 4:7).

Translation: *"You don't have to go down this path, Cain. But if you don't deal with what's building in you, it's going to deal with you."*

And it did.

The Nature of Shadows

Shadows aren't evil in themselves—they're evidence. They mean something's standing in the light but blocking it at the same time. In our lives, shadows show up as regrets, unhealed wounds, buried anger, or things left unsaid. Some shadows are private. Some are public. But either way, they shape how we move, relate, and respond.

Think about it: How many of your present habits are shaped by past pain? How many of your reactions today are based on something someone else did ten years ago? Shadows linger. And if they aren't addressed, they'll mislead you, mislabel others, and multiply dysfunction.

Jesus understood the danger of unresolved anger. In Matthew 5:21–22, He told His audience that anger left alone is just as deadly as murder. He wasn't saying the two were morally equal—He was saying the root of both is the same. If you don't check your heart, you'll live with your fists clenched. If you don't address the disappointment, you'll take it out on people who didn't cause it.

Shadows are like that. They don't just trail behind you—they stretch ahead of you too.

Jesus and the Better Brotherhood

But thank God, the story doesn't end with Cain. Because while Abel's blood cried out from the ground for justice, another blood was shed that cried out something better.

Hebrews 12:24 tells us that Jesus is "the mediator of a new covenant... whose sprinkled blood speaks a better word than the blood of Abel." Cain spilled Abel's blood out of jealousy. But Jesus spilled His blood out of love.
Jesus doesn't just redeem us from our past—He redefines what it means to be a brother. A real keeper. Not one who watches his brother suffer and walks away, but one who walks toward the wounded and says, "I've got you."

Jesus expanded that definition even further in Luke 10:25–37, when He told the parable of the Good Samaritan. A man is beaten and left for dead. Religious people see him, but they keep moving. Then a Samaritan—someone unexpected, even unwelcome—steps in. He doesn't preach a sermon. He doesn't throw a verse at him. He binds his wounds. He carries him. He pays for his recovery. And Jesus ends the story with a challenge: *"Go and do likewise."*

That's what brotherhood looks like. Not just shared bloodlines, but shared burdens. Not just proximity, but responsibility. You can't call yourself your brother's keeper and stay uninvolved in his pain. You can't claim faith and ignore the people in your life falling apart silently.

Jesus made this crystal clear in Matthew 5:43–44 when He said:

"You have heard that it was said, 'You shall love your neighbor and hate your enemy.' But I say to you, love your enemies and pray for those who persecute you."

That's a whole new level of brotherhood. That's not just keeping your friend—that's keeping even the one who doesn't want to be kept. That's leadership. That's maturity. That's Kingdom.

And it's not optional.

James 1:22 reminds us that if we only hear the Word but don't do it, we're deceiving ourselves. Being your brother's keeper isn't about big moments—it's about daily obedience. It's being willing to feed someone who's hungry, encourage someone who's drifting, or have a tough conversation when someone's walking off the rails.

Stepping Out of the Shadows

What kind of shadow are you casting? Are you the brother who avoids responsibility? Or the man who walks toward it? Have you let comparison turn into resentment? Or are you using someone else's win as inspiration, not intimidation? Are you still carrying what happened to you so heavily that you can't carry someone else?

Cain's question still lingers in our time: *"Am I my brother's keeper?"* (Genesis 4:9)

Yes. You are.

Through Christ, you don't have to be Cain. Through Christ, your story doesn't have to end with regret. You can be a builder. A protector. A brother. A keeper.

The Call to Reach Our Brothers

Brother, it's not enough to *not* harm your brother. You're called to go after him. To notice when he's distant. To ask the hard questions. To step in when it's easier to stay out. Because some men are bleeding spiritually, and no one's even asking where they are. Cain's failure wasn't just what he did; it was what he refused to take responsibility for.

Brotherhood isn't just a bond—it's a burden, a holy one. And too many men are bleeding spiritually while the rest of us walk by like it's none of our business. But it is. Because being your brother's keeper doesn't stop at the ones you already love—it includes the ones you're still called to reach.

Some of the men who need us most won't walk into a church. They won't pick up a Bible. They won't call for help. But they'll open up over a lunch break. They'll ask questions in the gym. They'll follow your consistency before they trust your theology. That's evangelism. That's witnessing. That's how we win them—not by shouting across the fence, but by walking across the street.

And we can't afford to wait until they're gone to realize they mattered.

Jesus didn't just call us to believe. He called us to *go*.

"Go therefore and make disciples of all the nations, baptizing them in the name of the Father and of the Son and of the Holy Spirit."
—Matthew 28:19

That's not a verse for missionaries. That's a mandate for men. For brothers. For you. And you will probably see this same scripture a few more times because it is just that important.

The first murder in Scripture wasn't just a tragedy—it was a warning. When we refuse to reach, we begin to resemble Cain. When we avoid the lost, we answer God's question the same way: "Am I my brother's keeper?" And the answer must be yes. Even when it's hard. Even when it's awkward. Even when we don't have all the answers.

Because someone once reached for you.

In a world where too many men are silently slipping through the cracks, your presence could be their lifeline. Your courage to speak, to invite, to share what saved you, could be the moment that saves them. You don't have to preach a sermon. You just have to open your mouth and care.

The question isn't, "Am I my brother's keeper?" The answer is already yes. The real question is, *Are you willing to go after him?*

As 2 Corinthians 5:17 says, "If anyone is in Christ, he is a new creation. The old has passed away; behold, the new has come."

That means your past doesn't define you. The shadows don't get the last word.

You do.

CHAPTER 2
The Unseen Bond

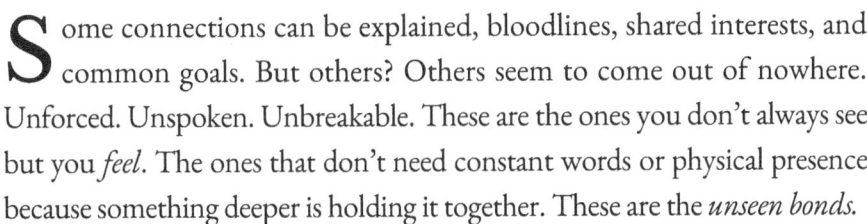

Some connections can be explained, bloodlines, shared interests, and common goals. But others? Others seem to come out of nowhere. Unforced. Unspoken. Unbreakable. These are the ones you don't always see but you *feel*. The ones that don't need constant words or physical presence because something deeper is holding it together. These are the *unseen bonds*.

Every man, at some point, has experienced this kind of connection, maybe with a childhood friend, a spiritual brother, or someone God placed in your life at just the right moment. And even if you've never had it, your soul still knows what it's missing.

That's because God designed us not just to be connected, but to be *spiritually tied*.

The Echo of Something Eternal

Unseen bonds are not fantasy. They are spiritual threads, woven by trust, loyalty, calling, and covenant. They show up in friendships that defy distance. In conversations that feel like home. In the kind of loyalty that doesn't flinch when things fall apart.

Think about the writer and their muse. There's no contract, no demand, just a pull, a rhythm, a knowing. Or the sailor and the sea, each wave speaking a language only one heart understands. These aren't romantic ideas. They're pictures of spiritual alignment. And that's what *The Unseen Bond* is about: the kind of relationship that isn't always seen, but it's *always real*.

You've heard the stories, of lifelong friends who reconnect after decades and pick up right where they left off. Or of two strangers from different worlds who somehow speak the same spiritual language. These aren't accidents. They're alignments. And Scripture gives us powerful examples of this kind of soul-knit connection.

David and Jonathan: A Paradigm of Spiritual Brotherhood

It all starts in **1 Samuel 18:1–4 (NLT)**:

"After David had finished talking with Saul, he met Jonathan, the king's son. There was an immediate bond between them, for Jonathan loved David.

From that day on Saul kept David with him and wouldn't let him return home. And Jonathan made a solemn pact with David, because he loved him as he loved himself. Jonathan sealed the pact by taking off his robe and giving it to David, together with his tunic, sword, bow, and belt."

From the moment David returned from slaying Goliath, something bigger than friendship sparked between him and Jonathan. The Bible says Jonathan's soul was *knit* to David's. That's not surface. That's spiritual. That's a covenant-level connection.

Jonathan wasn't just giving David a sword, he was laying down his own right to the throne. He wasn't just showing support, he was choosing to elevate David, even when it meant losing power himself. That's unseen bond loyalty. That's kingdom friendship.

This wasn't convenient. Jonathan's father, Saul, hated David. He wanted him dead. But Jonathan stayed loyal, not to politics, not to comfort, but to *purpose*. He warned David of danger. He covered him. He advocated for him. And when they parted ways, they wept, not because the bond was breaking, but because it was deeper than distance could touch.

There's a kind of brotherhood that's born in shared mission, godly trust, and spiritual respect. Jonathan didn't need David to be like him. He just needed David to walk with him. Their friendship wasn't casual, it was covenant. And every man needs at least one of those.

Jesus and His Disciples: The Ultimate Unseen Bond

If David and Jonathan show us the power of brotherhood, Jesus and His disciples show us the source of it. And within that circle, His relationship with John, *the disciple whom Jesus loved*, gives us a glimpse of divine closeness.

John 13:23 (NKJV) simply states, "Now there was leaning on Jesus' bosom one of His disciples, whom Jesus loved." That disciple was John. He wasn't the loudest in the group. He didn't walk on water. But he stayed close. At the table. At the cross. In the resurrection. While Peter was swinging swords and making declarations, John was staying still anchored in presence, not performance.

And when Jesus was breathing His last breath, it was John He entrusted His mother to (***John 19:26–27***). Not because John was biologically related, but because there was trust. There was a bond.

Jesus called all His disciple's "friends" in ***John 15:13–15***, saying:

"Greater love has no one than this, than to lay down one's life for his friends."

And then He did exactly that.

Jesus didn't just talk about unseen bonds, He bled for them. And in doing so, He taught us that the strongest connections are rooted not in shared history, but in sacrificial love.

The Bond in Today's World

Let's bring it forward.

We live in a time where relationships are often shallow, transactional, and built on convenience. People follow and unfollow. Show up when it's easy. Exit when it's hard. But spiritual bonds don't operate on convenience, they're anchored in commitment.

Proverbs 17:17 (NIV) says, *"A friend loves at all times, and a brother is born for a time of adversity."*

That's not just poetic. That's prophetic. A true brother shows up when it gets real. Not because it's expected, but because something in him *won't let him walk away.*

We all want that kind of connection. But the question is, are we willing to be that kind of brother?

Ecclesiastes 4:9–12 (NIV) gives us the blueprint:

> "Two are better than one, because they have a good return for their labor:
> If either of them falls down, one can help the other up.
> But pity anyone who falls and has no one to help them up...
> Though one may be overpowered, two can defend themselves.
> A cord of three strands is not quickly broken."

This isn't just about having someone to call. It's about being the one who helps the other up. It's about recognizing that spiritual brotherhood isn't weak—it's warfare. And you fight better when you're not alone.

Living the Unseen Bond

Galatians 6:2 (NIV) says, "Carry each other's burdens, and in this way you will fulfill the law of Christ."
That's real connection. That's love in motion.

You're not just called to be friendly—you're called to be present. To show up. To lift. To intercede. To check in. To speak truth in love. And to bear with one another when the weight gets heavy.

Unseen bonds don't announce themselves. But you'll know when you're walking in one. You'll feel it when a brother calls you out without tearing you down. When someone prays for you without asking for anything in return. When another man celebrates your win like it's his own.

That's what Jesus modeled. That's what David and Jonathan lived. That's what Scripture keeps calling us back to.

1 Peter 4:8–10 (NIV) says:

> "Above all, love each other deeply, because love covers over a multitude of sins.
> Offer hospitality to one another without grumbling.
> Each of you should use whatever gift you have received to serve others, as faithful stewards of God's grace in its various forms."

The unseen bond is where love meets loyalty. Where grace meets grit. Where commitment meets covenant.

You won't find it scrolling. You won't stumble into it by accident. You've got to build it. Guard it. Invest in it. And most importantly, you've got to *be* it.

Tied Together by Something Greater

An unseen bond isn't just a passing feeling or emotional spark. It's something rooted, anchored in the Spirit of God. It forms when faith is shared, when trust is earned, and when love proves itself in the form of sacrifice. These kinds of connections don't just build community—they build men. They build legacy. They build the kind of strength you can lean on when everything else falls apart.

This is the kind of bond that reminds you you're not walking alone. It's the quiet presence that holds you up when words fail. It's a brother who prays for you when you're too tired to speak. A friend who stays when the crowd walks out. A keeper who sees your flaws and still fights for your future.

When we live this way, we reflect the heart of God. We carry the kind of loyalty Jesus had for His disciples—the kind of love that washes feet and stays through the storm. We echo Jonathan, who laid down his own rights so his brother could rise. These unseen bonds may not always make headlines, but they hold up heaven's agenda here on earth.

They're not loud. But they're lasting.
They're not flashy. But they're faithful.
And in a world where people keep walking away, you choose to stay.

That's the unseen bond.
That's kingdom.
And it's yours to keep.

CHAPTER 3

Echoes of Brotherhood

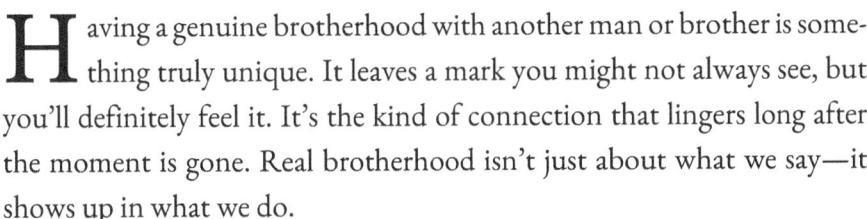

Having a genuine brotherhood with another man or brother is something truly unique. It leaves a mark you might not always see, but you'll definitely feel it. It's the kind of connection that lingers long after the moment is gone. Real brotherhood isn't just about what we say—it shows up in what we do.

In loyalty, brother.
In sacrifice.
In the willingness to give something up for someone else.

It's about choosing to walk together, not because we have to, but because we both feel that pull to do so. Scripture is full of examples where men didn't just stand on their own—they stood with someone. Not because they had to, but because *purpose* pulled them together.

Echoes of Brotherhood explores two powerful partnerships—Moses and Aaron in the Old Testament, and Peter and John in the New. These are not casual relationships. These are covenant connections built on a shared mission, divine calling, and spiritual trust. And their examples remind us that brotherhood isn't about biology. It's about belief, support, and walking in step with God's assignment—together.

Moses and Aaron: Complementing Strengths in Divine Mission

Moses didn't ask for the spotlight. When God called him at the burning bush, he hesitated. He questioned his ability, his voice, and his worthiness. But in Exodus 4:14–16 (NKJV), God answers his insecurity with a brother:

> "So the anger of the Lord was kindled against Moses, and He said: 'Is not Aaron the Levite your brother? I know that he can speak well. And look, he is also coming out to meet you. When he sees you, he will be glad in his heart.
> Now you shall speak to him and put the words in his mouth. And I will be with your mouth and with his mouth, and I will teach you what you shall do.
> So he shall be your spokesman to the people. And he himself shall be as a mouth for you, and you shall be to him as God.'"

God didn't change Moses' calling. He simply brought someone alongside him to help him carry it. Aaron wasn't just a backup. He was the complement—the mouthpiece to Moses' mission. The voice that carried the message Moses carried in his heart.

That's the echo of brotherhood—someone who doesn't take over your assignment, but helps you walk it out.

Aaron's role wasn't glamorous. He wasn't the one who parted the Red Sea. He wasn't the one who received the Ten Commandments. But his obedience made room for Moses' obedience to flourish. That's what true brothers do—they don't compete, they complete. They don't highlight your weaknesses—they strengthen them.

Every man needs an Aaron. And every man should be one. In moments when leadership feels overwhelming, when the mission feels bigger than our voice, God often sends someone not to replace us, but to run with us.

Peter and John: Unified by Faith and Purpose

"Now Peter and John went up together to the temple at the hour of prayer, the ninth hour. And a certain man lame from his mother's womb was carried, whom they laid daily at the gate of the temple which is called Beautiful, to ask alms from those who entered the temple; who, seeing Peter and John about to go into the temple, asked for alms.
And fixing his eyes on him, with John, Peter said, 'Look at us.'
So he gave them his attention, expecting to receive something from them.
Then Peter said, 'Silver and gold I do not have, but what I do have I give you: In the name of Jesus Christ of Nazareth, rise up and walk.'
And he took him by the right hand and lifted him up, and immediately his feet and ankle bones received strength.
So he, leaping up, stood and walked and entered the temple with them—walking, leaping, and praising God.
And all the people saw him walking and praising God.
Then they knew that it was he who sat begging alms at the Beautiful Gate of the temple; and they were filled with wonder and amazement at what had happened to him."
—Acts 3:1–10 (NKJV)

They weren't headed to perform miracles—they were going to pray. But when they saw the man sitting there, broken and begging, they didn't pass by. They didn't debate or delay. They moved *together*. Peter spoke up—clear, certain, full of faith. And John? He didn't need to say a word. He stood there, steady. Present.

That healing didn't come from Peter alone. It flowed through unity. Through brotherhood. That's what happens when men show up together—one leads, the other covers. That's strength. That's trust. That's what it looks like when brothers walk in step with the Spirit.
One mission. One moment. One goal.
And a miracle that shouted louder than either of them could've said alone.

Peter and John share a brotherhood that extends beyond this singular act, permeating their joint efforts in spreading the Gospel. Their story shows how much we can achieve when we come together with others who believe in the same purpose and commitment to what really matters: our faith and dedication to God's mission.

That's what brotherhood looks like in action—not just being there when it's easy, but being in sync when it's spiritual. When Peter and John moved together, people noticed. The man walked. The crowd gathered. And the Gospel spread.

Their brotherhood didn't stop at that gate. They stood side by side in prison. They faced opposition together. They defended their faith together. And they strengthened the early Church—*together*.

Who's walking with you to the temple?
Who sees what you see, believes what you believe, and is bold enough to take the next step with you?
Better yet, who are you standing beside?

A Brotherhood That Resonates Today

These stories aren't just ancient records—they're living blueprints. Moses and Aaron. Peter and John. They teach us something vital: brotherhood echoes when we share the burden, carry the mission, and protect the purpose.

Proverbs 27:17 (NKJV) reminds us, "As iron sharpens iron, so a man sharpens the countenance of his friend."
Brotherhood is not soft. It's strong. It's necessary. It's the sound of one man helping another be more of who God created him to be.

Ecclesiastes 4:9–10 (NIV) puts it this way:

> "Two are better than one, because they have a good return for their labor.

If either of them falls down, one can help the other up.
But pity anyone who falls and has no one to help them up."

That's the weight of this calling. Brotherhood isn't just about having company—it's about having a covenant. It's about knowing that when you fall, someone's reaching out—not just to pull you up, but to walk with you forward.

And when we echo that kind of brotherhood in our lives, our homes get stronger. Our churches get sharper. Our communities get safer. Not because we're perfect, but because we're present.

One Shared Mission, Many Voices

What Moses and Aaron shared wasn't about one man's gifts being better than the other—it was about both voices moving in the same direction. What Peter and John displayed wasn't about titles or spotlight—it was about faith in agreement.

That's what we need more of today. Men who know how to speak **with** one another, not **over** one another. Brothers who understand that the mission of Christ is always bigger than the ego of man.

Galatians 6:2 (NIV) says, "Carry each other's burdens, and in this way you will fulfill the law of Christ."

That's brotherhood.
That's weight-sharing.
That's Gospel.

And in a world full of noise, betrayal, and breakdown, *Echoes of Brotherhood* invites us to live differently—to link arms with someone in faith, to cover each other in prayer, to walk boldly into purpose, and to let our united steps speak louder than any sermon ever could.

CHAPTER 4

Guardian of Secrets

The sacred tension between what's hidden and what's revealed runs through the center of every believer's journey. It's in that space—between secrecy and truth—that much of our faith, our pain, and our growth is shaped. Some secrets protect. Others divide. Some heal. Others haunt. But one thing remains certain: secrets mark us.

The Bible doesn't shy away from tension. It shows us how sometimes things had to stay hidden for a season so purpose could rise at the right time. And when the truth finally came out, it didn't just shift a moment; it changed everything in the future. Look at Joseph. Look at Jesus. Two men who walked through betrayal, carried things they couldn't talk about, waited for God's timing, and still chose forgiveness when they had every reason not to. Their paths weren't clean or easy—but they were redemptive. And as we trace their stories, we don't just see what happened—we start to see ourselves: what we've buried, what we've carried, and what God's been building the whole time.

Guardian of Secrets is more than a title—it's a call. Each of us, at one point or another, is entrusted with truths we don't fully understand, stories we haven't finished living, and pain we've never spoken about. The question we must wrestle with is this: **What will we do with what we carry?**

Jesus didn't reveal His identity all at once. Throughout the Gospels, we see Him intentionally navigating the space between what He concealed and what He chose to unveil—especially in moments like His conversation with the Samaritan woman at the well. Revelation, in His hands, wasn't just information—it was transformation. It opened the door to salvation, challenged assumptions, and invited people into something deeper.

In the same way, the life of Joseph reveals the weight of hidden truth and the healing that can follow when that truth is revealed with wisdom. These stories echo the same theme: **divine timing matters.** Secrets, when surrendered to God, can lead to reconciliation, healing, and redemption.

Whether through Joseph's long path to forgiveness or Jesus' quiet unveiling of grace, we're reminded that secrecy, revelation, and restoration aren't just biblical ideas—they're deeply human. We all carry things. And eventually, God calls us to confront what we carry—not to crush us, but to grow us. Because the secrets we hold often shape the story God wants to tell.

The Secret That Shaped a Story

Joseph's journey didn't start in a palace—it started in a pit. And it wasn't dug by enemies. It was dug by brothers.

He was the dreamer. The favored one. The kid with the coat. He spoke of visions—of sheaves and stars bowing down—and his brothers couldn't handle it.

Genesis 37:28 (NLT) captures the weight of their betrayal:

> "So when the Ishmaelites, who were Midianite traders, came by, Joseph's brothers pulled him out of the cistern and sold him to them for twenty pieces of silver. And the traders took him to Egypt."

That moment—the shove into the pit, the silver exchanged, the coat dipped in blood—wasn't just about jealousy. It was the beginning of a secret that would ripple through a family for decades.

And Joseph? He carried the weight of that silence into slavery, into prison, and into Pharaoh's court. But here's the thing: what was hidden didn't stop God's plan. It became the soil for something greater.

The Rise of the Keeper

Joseph didn't climb his way to the top. He was dragged down first... betrayed by blood, locked away by lies, and left behind in prison by people who forgot his name. But through every pit and every prison, he didn't crack. He adjusted. Grew. Stayed faithful. And even when it looked like no one saw him, God never left his side.

Then came the shift. Pharaoh had a dream nobody could decode. Every voice in Egypt fell silent—except one. Joseph. The same man they tried to bury now had the answer no one else could give. And when he opened his mouth, what came out wasn't revenge. It was clarity, purpose, and direction. The one who had been silenced stepped up with authority. Because that's what happens when you stay faithful in the dark. God raises you up to lead when the lights come on.

Genesis 41:39-40 (NLT) records Pharaoh's words:

> "Since God has revealed the meaning of the dreams to you, clearly no one else is as intelligent or wise as you are.
> You will be in charge of my court, and all my people will take orders from you. Only I, sitting on my throne, will have a rank higher than yours."

Just like that, Joseph went from prisoner to prime minister. From forgotten to favored. But the story wasn't finished. Because the same brothers who sold him were about to show up—starving, desperate, and unaware that their secret was about to be confronted.

Joseph had every right to retaliate. To expose. To punish. But instead, he tested. He waited. He observed. And when the moment was right, he revealed.

When Secrets Weep

Genesis 45:1–5 (NLT) brings us into the raw center of the story:

> "Joseph could stand it no longer. There were many people in the room, and he said to his attendants, 'Out, all of you!' So he was alone with his brothers when he told them who he was.
> Then he broke down and wept. He wept so loudly the Egyptians could hear him, and word of it quickly carried to Pharaoh's palace.
> 'I am Joseph!' he said to his brothers. 'Is my father still alive?'
> But his brothers were speechless! They were stunned to realize that Joseph was standing there in front of them.
> 'Please, come closer,' he said to them. So they came closer. And he said again, 'I am Joseph, your brother, whom you sold into slavery in Egypt.
> But don't be upset, and don't be angry with yourselves for selling me to this place. It was God who sent me here ahead of you to preserve your lives.'"

This wasn't just a family reunion. It was a release. Of pain. Of years lost. Of secrets kept. And the most powerful part? Joseph didn't use the truth to wound. He used it to restore.

That's the mark of a guardian—not just someone who carries secrets, but someone who knows when and how to reveal them for the sake of redemption.

Jesus: The Hidden Messiah

Now shift the lens to the New Testament: a different story, a different time, but the same divine rhythm of concealment and revelation.

Jesus didn't walk into His ministry shouting His identity. He wasn't out to prove Himself in flashy ways. Instead, He revealed who He was—bit by bit, moment by moment, heart by heart.

One of those moments happened at a well with a woman the world had written off.

In John 4:25–26 (NLT):

> "The woman said, 'I know the Messiah is coming—the one who is called Christ. When he comes, he will explain everything to us.' Then Jesus told her, 'I am the Messiah!'"

He didn't make that announcement to a king. Or a crowd. He made it to a Samaritan woman with a broken past and a thirsty soul.

Why? Because truth isn't always for the platform. Sometimes, it's for the person ready to receive it. Jesus, like Joseph, didn't reveal Himself to shame, but to save.

The Power of Forgiveness and Revelation

What connects Joseph and Jesus isn't just that they both held secrets—it's what they did when they revealed them.

Joseph didn't crush his brothers. He comforted them.
Jesus didn't condemn the world. He offered salvation.

Both showed us that forgiveness isn't forgetting—it's choosing grace over revenge. It's seeing God's hand in the harm. It's understanding that sometimes, the very thing meant to destroy you becomes the platform God uses to elevate you.

Luke 23:34 (NKJV) records Jesus' words on the cross: "Father, forgive them, for they do not know what they do."

That's the heart of a guardian. Not just someone who holds back, but someone who gives grace when it's least expected and most needed.

What Are You Guarding?

Let's bring it home.

What are the secrets you're carrying?
What truth have you buried because you're afraid of what it might change?
What grace are you withholding because someone else doesn't "deserve" it?

We've all been there—carrying things that feel too heavy, hiding wounds that feel too deep, waiting for the right moment to come clean. But here's the thing: what's hidden in you can't heal you. And what you're protecting might be the very thing God wants to use.

The stories of Joseph and Jesus show us that timing matters. That healing takes wisdom. That revelation requires courage. But most of all, they show us that grace has the final word.

Nothing Wasted

In God's hands, no detail is wasted. No betrayal is pointless. No silence is empty.

Joseph's pit wasn't the end—it was the beginning of purpose.
Jesus' silence before Pilate wasn't a weakness—it was strategy.

Your pain? Your secrecy? Your story? God sees it. And He knows how to use it.

Romans 8:28 (NKJV) says it best: "And we know that all things work together for good to those who love God, to those who are the called according to His purpose."

That's the anthem of the guardian. That's the testimony of the kept. That's the legacy of those who know how to carry what God gives—and release it when the time is right.

Guarding with Grace

You're not called to be silent forever. And you're not called to blurt out the truth recklessly. You're called to walk in wisdom. To speak when the Spirit says speak. To forgive when your flesh wants revenge. To restore when others would run.

To be a guardian of secrets is not just to carry weight—it's to bear it well.

That means...

- Being trusted with someone else's truth and not using it as a weapon
- Knowing when to hold your peace and when to speak up in love
- Choosing to see God's hand even in the hurt
- Letting your story point to His glory

The Final Reveal

One day, every secret will be revealed. Every hidden motive. Every buried pain. Every unseen act of faithfulness. And on that day, the only thing that will matter is whether we lived as guardians of God's grace or as prisoners of our own pain.

Joseph forgave. Jesus forgave. And now, it's our turn.

So ask yourself:
What have I been holding onto?
Who needs my forgiveness?
What secret in me is ready to be surrendered so God can do something greater?

Tony Austin Jr.

Because when you walk like Joseph...
And love like Jesus...
You're not just guarding secrets.
You're carrying the keys to healing.

CHAPTER 5

Shared Paths, Divergent Journeys

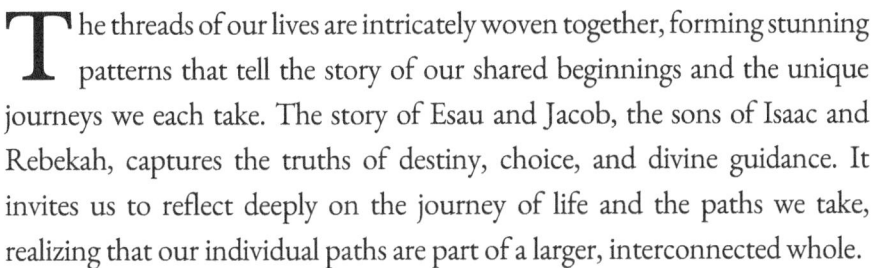

The threads of our lives are intricately woven together, forming stunning patterns that tell the story of our shared beginnings and the unique journeys we each take. The story of Esau and Jacob, the sons of Isaac and Rebekah, captures the truths of destiny, choice, and divine guidance. It invites us to reflect deeply on the journey of life and the paths we take, realizing that our individual paths are part of a larger, interconnected whole.

> "And the Lord told her, 'The sons in your womb will become two nations. From the very beginning, the two nations will be rivals. One nation will be stronger than the other; and your older son will serve your younger son.'
> And when the time came to give birth, Rebekah discovered that she did indeed have twins! The first one was very red at birth and covered with thick hair like a fur coat. So they named him Esau. Then the other twin was born with his hand grasping Esau's heel. So they named him Jacob. Isaac was sixty years old when the twins were born."
> —Genesis 25:23–34

The scripture above doesn't just introduce two brothers—it draws a contrast between two paths. From the womb, Esau and Jacob were on a collision course with destiny. Esau came out first: rugged, impulsive, and driven by the moment. A man of the hunt, strong and physical. Jacob followed, hand on his brother's heel, steady and intentional. Not one for the field, but for the firelight of the tent. He was wired for thought, not thrill—reflection, not reaction.

What we see in these two is more than personality differences. It's a picture of how values shape vision, and how choices shape the course of a life.

Then comes the moment. Esau stumbles in from the wilderness, weary and famished. Jacob sees an opening. A pot of stew becomes a test of perspective. Esau gave up more than a meal that day—he gave up meaning. He let a temporary appetite rob him of a permanent inheritance. It wasn't just a bite of stew. It was a forfeiture of identity, legacy, and spiritual position.

Jacob saw what Esau missed.

He recognized the weight of what was on the table—not the stew, but the stake. And while the moment may seem unfair, it reveals something deeper: one man surrendered his future to satisfy a feeling; the other seized a moment that would change the narrative of his bloodline.

And brothers, that story isn't ancient history—it's happening now, not in tents or deserts, but in our lives. It happens when we choose comfort over calling. When we let our cravings override our convictions. When we trade depth for dopamine.

Because sometimes, the decisions that feel harmless in the moment leave generational consequences. The stew might have solved a craving, but it cost Esau a calling. That's the danger of living for the immediate. You can end up forfeiting the irreversible. The truth is, every man comes to a decision point—a moment where his character will be tested for convenience. And whether it's five minutes or five months, what you say yes to now can set the course for what God does next.

So before you hand over what's sacred for what's easy, stop and ask: *Is this filling a hunger, or feeding my future?*

This passage doesn't exist to entertain. It exists to awaken. It reminds us that not every appetite should be fed. That not every shortcut is harmless. And that some trades don't just cost us—they echo long after we're gone.

Brother, what are you holding onto? And more importantly... what are you giving up without realizing it?

Incorporating biblical scriptures, the narrative extends beyond these brothers to reflect a universal theme: the journey of life, with its shared beginnings and divergent paths, is a complex interplay of individual choices and divine orchestration.

> "This son was our ancestor Isaac. When he married Rebekah, she gave birth to twins. But before they were born, before they had done anything good or bad, she received a message from God. (This message shows that God chooses people according to his own purposes; he calls people, but not according to their good or bad works.)
> She was told, 'Your older son will serve your younger son.'
> In the words of the Scriptures, 'I loved Jacob, but I rejected Esau.'"
> —Romans 9:10–13 (NLT)

The Apostle Paul reflects in Romans 9:10–13 on a truth that cuts deeper than birth order or human effort: God chooses according to His own purpose. Before Esau and Jacob were even born—before they had done anything good or bad—God already spoke. Not based on performance, but on purpose. He declared, "The older will serve the younger." And Paul reminds us, "Jacob I loved, but Esau I rejected." These verses don't reflect bias—they reveal a blueprint. Paul is pointing to something bigger than fairness: divine intention. God doesn't make decisions based on what we think makes sense. He moves according to His purpose, not our preferences.

Jacob and Esau weren't just brothers—they were a picture of two directions a man can take. From birth, their lives moved in separate rhythms. One lived driven by appetite; the other by instinct for something more. And it wasn't luck that shaped them—it was what they responded to. One traded legacy for relief. The other walked a longer road, but he walked with purpose. Their story isn't just history—it's a map, because every man stands at that same invisible fork. Not just once, but often. And where you end up has more to do with your daily choices than your starting point. Who you listen to, what you reach for, and when you decide to grow up—all of it counts.

Because what we chase shapes who we become. Conviction matters, direction matters. And so does the discipline to pursue what God placed in front of us—especially when it costs us comfort. And what we pursue reveals what we truly value. And the more we sit with it, the more we realize: this isn't just history—it's a mirror.

Esau was born first and built for the outdoors—a man's man, strong, immediate, and physical. Jacob followed, hand on heel, contemplative, strategic, steady. From the beginning, their differences weren't just personality traits—they were prophetic clues. One chased the hunt. The other carried the promise.

Then comes the defining moment. Hunger meets opportunity. Esau trades his birthright for a bowl of stew. What should've been sacred became disposable. And in doing so, he chose the moment over the mission.

And that's where this story hits us, because every man faces these kinds of trades. Maybe not over stew, but over a decision that could cost him his legacy. One click. One compromise. One shortcut. One grudge held too long. The question isn't, "Will you face a trade?" The question is, "Will you know what it's really costing you?"

Jacob's journey wasn't clean. He wrestled. He deceived. He ran. But God still had His hand on him. And even in Jacob's mess, there was a message. God doesn't wait for perfect men—He works through surrendered ones. And when Jacob finally yielded, God didn't just change his direction. He changed his name. *Israel.* He went from heel-grabber to nation-builder.

That's what this chapter is calling out of you. The part of you that's been chasing approval, performance, or shortcuts. The part of you that's forgotten there's a birthright at stake. But here's the good news: it's not too late to value what God placed on your life. It's not too late to reclaim the path you almost sold for something that couldn't feed your future.

God's sovereignty doesn't cancel your choices, but it will redeem them if you return. So let Jacob and Esau's story be more than a Sunday school lesson. Let it be a wake-up call. To see the value of what's in your hands. To stop feeding temporary hunger. And to trust that even when you've wandered, there's still a way home.

The greatest legacy isn't built on impulse; it's built on identity—knowing who you are in God and walking like it. Every day. Every decision. Every moment.

> "Train up a child in the way he should go [teaching him to seek God's wisdom and will for his abilities and talents]. Even when he is old he will not depart from it."
> —Proverbs 22:6 (AMP)

The path Jacob walked wasn't just marked by conflict—it was marked by a personal encounter. That night at Bethel, when heaven opened and a ladder stretched from earth to glory, Jacob didn't just see angels—he saw the truth. God wasn't far off. He was involved. Present. Engaged. That ladder wasn't a spectacle; it was a statement: there is more going on than what you see. Heaven speaks. Earth moves. And when a man listens, everything shifts.

Jacob's dream reminds us that God doesn't wait for perfect places—He meets us in hard ones. That encounter in the wilderness became an altar. And for every man still wrestling between where he is and where he's called to be, that's the kind of God we follow. One who shows up. One who speaks. One who still builds altars in the middle of nowhere.

> "Meanwhile, Jacob left Beersheba and traveled toward Haran. At sundown he arrived at a good place to set up camp and stopped there for the night. Jacob found a stone to rest his head against and lay down to sleep.
> As he slept, he dreamed of a stairway that reached from the earth up to heaven. And he saw the angels of God going up and down the stairway.
> At the top of the stairway stood the Lord, and he said, 'I am the Lord, the God of your grandfather Abraham, and the God of your father, Isaac. The ground you are lying on belongs to you. I am giving it to you and your descendants.
> Your descendants will be as numerous as the dust of the earth! They will spread out in all directions—to the west and the east, to the north and the south. And all the families of the earth will be blessed through you and your descendants.
> What's more, I am with you, and I will protect you wherever you go. One day I will bring you back to this land. I will not leave you until I have finished giving you everything I have promised you.'
> Then Jacob awoke from his sleep and said, 'Surely the Lord is in this place, and I wasn't even aware of it!'
> But he was also afraid and said, 'What an awesome place this is! It is none other than the house of God, the very gateway to heaven!'"
> —Genesis 28:10–17

Jacob didn't meet God in the comfort of a church pew, in an office cubicle, or sitting by the dock of the bay. He met Him on the run—with a rock for a pillow, regret in his chest, and the weight of bad choices catching up to him fast. He wasn't chasing revival. He was chasing relief.

And that's exactly where heaven showed up.

That ladder wasn't some divine decoration dropped into the scene for flair—it was God's way of saying, "I haven't backed out on you. I'm still reaching." It wasn't about Jacob finding God; it was about God finding Jacob, right in the middle of the mess.

Because that's who He is. He meets men in places where survival feels louder than faith. And He reminds them: *You're still part of the plan.*

Jacob's path wasn't straight, and it definitely wasn't clean. But it was purposeful.

From the start, his life reflected tension. Born second yet called first. His grip on Esau's heel at birth wasn't just symbolic—it was prophetic. Jacob didn't just want a blessing. He wanted what was destined, even if it didn't come easy, even if it came through struggle.

His journey from grasping to standing is filled with both divine encounters and gritty decisions. He didn't just inherit a legacy—he wrestled his way into one. From the vision of a ladder reaching from earth to heaven in Genesis 28, to the night he wrestled an angel and wouldn't let go until something changed (Genesis 32:24–28), Jacob's story is one of transformation. Not instant. Not painless. But real.

He went from Jacob, the deceiver, to Israel, the one who contends with God and prevails. That shift wasn't just about a name. It was about identity. Calling. Purpose. He didn't walk away the same. He walked away with a limp... and a legacy.

But his story doesn't end with him.

It extends through the life of his son, Joseph—a young man marked by favor but forged through rejection. Sold by his brothers, thrown into a pit, forgotten in a prison. Yet, in every season, God was present. In Genesis 37–50, we see Joseph rise, not just to power, but to perspective. While others saw loss, God was setting up legacy. Joseph tells his brothers in Genesis 50:20, "You intended to harm me, but God intended it for good." That's not just hindsight—that's heaven's view.

It echoes in the words of Romans 8:28, "And we know that all things work together for good to those who love God, to those who are called according to His purpose."

That's not a feel-good quote—it's a foundation. It means even when you don't see the pattern, God's weaving purpose is still there.

And this same thread of redemption shows up again in the parable of the prodigal son (Luke 15:11–32). A son who walks away, spends his inheritance, hits rock bottom, and still finds open arms. Not because he earned his way back, but because he remembered where home was. That's the power of a father's love. Of restoration. Of returning.

You see, these aren't just stories of individuals. They're portraits of us. Of men trying to figure it out. Of brothers who fall and fathers who forgive. Of sons who walk away and sons who wrestle, and of a God who stays constant through it all.

Jacob shows us that struggle doesn't disqualify you—it shapes you.

Joseph reminds us that favor doesn't mean easy—it means you're trusted with weight.

And the prodigal proves that no matter how far you've run, it's never too far to come back.

These lives weren't linear. They were layered. Their stories weren't clean. They weren't easy. They were stained with decisions that cost them something—sometimes everything. But they were never abandoned. That's the beauty of walking with God—He doesn't exit when the story gets complicated.

So, let's make this plain: God is not waiting on a flawless résumé. He's looking for men who won't quit when it gets dark. Suppose you've failed, fought, or fallen—good. That means you've lived. That means there's something for God to work with.

Your limp? It just means you've wrestled.
Your scar? Proof you survived.
Your past? It's not a closed door—it's evidence that grace reached you anyway.

So get up. Keep going. Stay in it.
Because God's not asking you to be perfect—He's asking you to keep walking.

Because the truth is, God doesn't waste the detour. He works through it. And if you're still moving, still showing up, still breathing, that means He's still building something in you.

So don't stop. Don't fold. Please don't give up because it's hard, slow, or unclear.
Just keep walking. He's not finished.

Because the same God who showed up at Bethel, the same God who sat with Joseph in a prison cell, the same God who ran toward a broken son, is still moving in your story.
He's not done with you yet.

> "Being confident of this very thing, that He who has begun a good work in you will complete it until the day of Jesus Christ."
> —Philippians 1:6 (NKJV)

Through this examination of these brothers, we come to appreciate that our journeys, though diverse, are interconnected in the vast expanse of human experience and divine interaction. The divergent paths of Esau and Jacob—and indeed all of us—are not merely individual trajectories, but are integral to the unfolding of a larger story that encompasses the shared and the unique, the temporal and the eternal. Through our personal journeys, or collectively as the body of Christ, or in your individual ministry—this isn't just their story, it's ours too.

Because deep down, every man is searching for something. For purpose. For identity. For a reason that outlives the grind. And whether we admit it or not, we're all hoping to find that in the presence of something—or Someone—greater than us.

So when we look at Esau and Jacob, we're not just reading history. We're looking into a mirror. We're being asked to pause and think: **What road am I really on?**

What choices are shaping my life? And am I letting God guide me, or am I trying to write the story by myself?

Because the truth is, He's already been in the details. And He's still willing to walk with you through whatever comes next. In doing so, we engage with the timeless dialogue between free will and wisdom, between our plans and those of God the sovereign One, enriching our journey with depth, purpose, and the potential for transformation.

There are brothers all around you—some who've wandered, others who were pushed out. Maybe they started on the same path you did. But now they're caught in cycles, shame, or silence. Don't just thank God you made it out. Go back. Reach for them. Walk a mile down their road if that's what it takes.

Evangelism isn't just for the gifted—it's the mandate of every man who's been redeemed. Jesus didn't save you so you could play it safe. He saved you to be sent.

> "Therefore, go and make disciples of all the nations, baptizing them in the name of the Father and the Son and the Holy Spirit."
> —Matthew 28:19 (NLT)

Some men won't walk into a church. But they'll walk with you. And *that* walk might be what leads them home.

You might be the only sermon they ever hear. The only Bible they'll ever read. They may not respond to a pulpit, but they'll pay attention to your peace. They may not know the difference between Genesis and John, but they'll notice how you handle stress, how you love your family, and how you talk when no one's watching.

You're not just living for yourself—you're living as a bridge. And sometimes, that bridge looks like a ride to work. A simple lunch. A "you good?" text that turns into a life-changing conversation. Sometimes it's not a full gospel presentation—it's just being consistent, showing up, and staying present.

Brother, don't underestimate what God can do through your witness—not with a title, but with your testimony. Not in a sanctuary, but in a barbershop. In the gym. On the job. In the silence of a shared struggle.

Because evangelism isn't always loud—sometimes it's just real. Just steady. Just faithful. And one day, that man walking beside you may look up and realize you weren't just walking with him—you were walking him back to Jesus.

CHAPTER 6

In the Mirror of Memory

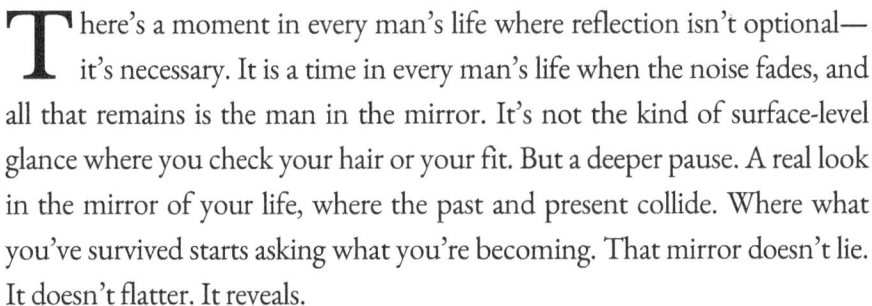

There's a moment in every man's life where reflection isn't optional—it's necessary. It is a time in every man's life when the noise fades, and all that remains is the man in the mirror. It's not the kind of surface-level glance where you check your hair or your fit. But a deeper pause. A real look in the mirror of your life, where the past and present collide. Where what you've survived starts asking what you're becoming. That mirror doesn't lie. It doesn't flatter. It reveals.

And in that reflection, you're met with the faces of those you've helped, those you've hurt, and those you've lost along the way. The wounds that haven't healed. The prayers you haven't prayed. The calling you've avoided. The love you've withheld. The forgiveness you've delayed. The brother you dropped. The grudge you carry. All of it stares back—not to shame, but to awaken.

David knew that mirror. In Psalm after Psalm, he didn't perform—he poured out. Not to impress anyone, but because the weight of his thoughts needed somewhere to land. In Psalm 139, he prays, "Search me, O God, and know my heart... see if there is any offensive way in me."

That's not performance. That's exposure. That's a man inviting God into his inner world—not to rearrange the furniture, but to tear down the walls.

But this kind of reflection isn't passive. It's not for the overly emotional or the deeply broken. It's for every man. Especially the one who thinks he's past that kind of vulnerability. Because the mirror doesn't just show what's behind you—it shows what's beneath you. What you've buried. What you've hidden behind your grind, your pride, or your silence.

And the truth is, when you finally stand still long enough to look back, you're not just facing regret—you're reclaiming authority. You're saying: *I won't let the past define me, but I will let it refine me.* Because every scar has a story, and every story has a reason. But healing doesn't start with a new chapter—it begins with an honest reflection.

This is not about reliving old pain. It's about confronting what's been quietly shaping your manhood without your permission. It's about asking God to show you not just where you've been, but who He still sees in you.

The Memory That Heals

David knew something about facing himself. Long before he was king, before the songs, before the crown, he was a shepherd boy with a slingshot and a soul full of songs. His Psalms weren't public statements. The Psalms weren't just poetic verses. They were gut-level honesty. Unedited cries. Sacred journals of a man in process. They were the sounds of a man digging through his memory and finding God in the middle of his mess.

> "The Lord is my shepherd; I lack nothing... He restores my soul..."
> —Psalm 23:1–3

Those aren't the words of a man who's never been broken. They're the confession of someone who's lost his way and found his God again.

Memory can heal when you allow it to be filtered through redemption. But it can also haunt you when you avoid it. Some of us are afraid to look back because we think it will undo us. But God never asks you to revisit your past to torment you. He brings it up to transform you. The wounds you hide are often the very places He wants to restore.

Healing doesn't happen by pretending; it happens by remembering and then releasing. It's confessing where it hurts. It's owning what you've buried. It's letting God clean out what you've tried to cover up. That's where freedom begins—not in denial, but in surrender.

And sometimes that healing doesn't come from a miracle moment—it comes through brotherhood. Through opening up to the men you trust. Through telling the truth to someone who's not there to fix you but to walk with you. Because when memory becomes shared, not secret, it begins to lose its sting.

The Mirror and the Garden

Jesus had His own mirror moment in the Garden of Gethsemane. He wasn't looking into a physical mirror, but He was staring straight into His assignment. And it brought Him to His knees. He saw the weight of what was ahead. The betrayal. The isolation. The cross.

And what did He say?

> "My soul is overwhelmed with sorrow to the point of death...
> My Father, if it is possible, may this cup be taken from me. Yet not as I will, but as You will."
> —Matthew 26:38–39

That's a man anchored in something greater. That's the sound of a man facing His destiny with honest emotion and unshakable resolve. It was the collision of humanity and divinity. Emotion and obedience. Sorrow and strength. And He didn't run from the mirror—He knelt in front of it. And then, He rose to fulfill what He was called to do.

Men, we all need a Gethsemane. A place where we come face to face with what God's asked of us. A place where we remember why we're here and who we're doing it for. Not to get stuck, but to get clarity. To wrestle honestly. To walk forward courageously. That's where real strength is formed.

Identity, Calling, and the Questions We Don't Ask

Every man carries questions he's afraid to voice:
"Am I enough?"
"Have I done too much damage to be used?"
"Can I still become who I was meant to be?"
The answer? Yes—through Jesus.

Your identity isn't in your past—it's in your position. Not your résumé, but your redemption. And that's why memory can become a mirror of mercy. Because when you reflect with the right lens, you stop seeing just mistakes and start seeing miracles. You know where you should've died, but didn't. You see what tried to break you, but built you instead. You see the hand of God in places you didn't even know He was working.

That's when calling starts to make sense. Not as a title, but as a testimony. Not as a role, but as a responsibility. God doesn't call you because you're polished—He calls you because you're purposed. And if you're still breathing, you're still called.

Brotherhood in the Mirror

No man becomes who he's supposed to be alone.
David had Jonathan.
Paul had Silas.
Moses had Aaron.
Even Jesus had the three in the garden with Him.

And you? You need brothers too.

Sometimes brotherhood means telling a man the truth he doesn't want to hear. Sometimes it's just showing up. Sometimes it's sitting in silence beside a man who's grieving and reminding him that he's not alone. Sometimes it's praying for him when he can't pray for himself.

The mirror isn't meant to be faced solo. You need a brother beside you. Not to tell you who you are—but to remind you when you forget.

And if you've never had that kind of brother, be that kind of brother. Start the healing cycle. Show the next man what faithfulness looks like.

Reflections That Call You Higher

You won't always like what the mirror shows. But if you let God speak through it, it will grow you.

You'll see the pride you need to lay down.
The apology you still need to make.
The son you need to call.
The dream you need to dust off.
The brother you need to forgive.
The fear you need to confront.
The God you need to trust.

Because that mirror isn't meant to shame you; it's meant to shape you. And what you do with what you see—that's where your manhood matures, your faith deepens, and your influence begins to speak. The man who walks away from the mirror unchanged loses more than clarity—he loses opportunity. But the one who leans in? Who remembers and repents? Who stands tall and walks forward? That man changes everything.

The Mirror Isn't the End

Brother, the mirror isn't your enemy. It's your invitation. Because in the mirror of memory, God doesn't take you backward to leave you there—He takes you back to build you better.

To go back and recover what you dropped.
To rise again from what you buried.
Walking with greater conviction.
Loving with greater compassion.
Leading with greater purpose.
Living with greater truth.

> "But if you look carefully into the perfect law that sets you free, and if you do what it says and don't forget what you heard, then God will bless you for doing it."
> —James 1:25 (NLT)

Not just for you, but for the ones coming behind you. Your sons. Your brothers. The men you lead. The people who draw strength from your example. Because the mirror doesn't just reflect what's broken—it reveals what's possible. It exposes what still hurts, but also what still lives.

So stand in front of it, not with shame, but with courage. Let it remind you of how far God has brought you, and how much more He still plans to do.

Because in the mirror of memory… grace still speaks, purpose still breathes, and God is still turning your scars into strategy.

CHAPTER 7

Unspoken Understandings

Some of the deepest connections you'll ever have won't be loud. They won't need a roundtable, a therapist, or a broadcast. They'll be lived. Felt. Proved. These are the relationships where trust doesn't have to shout—it just stands.

In the life of every man, there will be moments when your value is measured not by how much you say, but by how deeply you're trusted. In the Word, few stories display that quiet depth like the household of Mary, Martha, and Lazarus. Their bond with Jesus wasn't just personal—it was purposeful. It was intimate without being showy. Solid without a single sound needing to be made.

Sometimes, the greatest honor God can give a man is not a public assignment but a private trust.

A Brother's Trust: Mary, Martha, Lazarus, and a Mother's Insight

In John 11, we find the siblings Mary and Martha reaching out to Jesus about their brother Lazarus, who is sick. They send word, not with instructions or begging, but with a simple message: "Lord, the one you love is sick." No demands. No manipulation. Just a trust that Jesus would move because He cared. And He did—just not immediately.

Jesus waits, not out of neglect, but out of divine timing. He tells the disciples, "This sickness will not end in death. No, it is for God's glory so that God's Son may be glorified through it." —John 11:4

Now imagine that for a moment as a man—your friend delays. Your brother dies. You bury him. And still, you leave space for God to be God.

That's what trust looks like when it has history. You've seen Him work before, so you don't need a loud confirmation. You know He's moving, even if it doesn't feel like it. For Martha, this wasn't blind faith—it was built faith. "I know even now, God will give you whatever you ask." —John 11:22
That's trust forged in fellowship. Not forced. And for Mary? She doesn't say much. She weeps. She falls at His feet. She doesn't repeat the same question hoping for a better answer. She brings her grief. And Jesus meets her in it.

Because here's what this moment tells us: real trust doesn't always speak. But it always shows up.

In the same breath, you see the strength of Martha's declaration and the sorrow of Mary's silence. Jesus receives both. And He responds to both.

"Jesus wept." —John 11:35

It's the shortest verse in the Bible, but it's one of the most powerful. Why? Because it proves that God doesn't just respond to language—He responds to love. And when He sees a heart breaking in faith, He moves.

The Wedding at Cana: A Mother's Nudge, A Son's Power

Then there's Jesus and His mother in John 2—the wedding at Cana. The wine runs out, and Mary doesn't make a scene. She comes to Jesus with a statement:

"They have no more wine."

Jesus replies, "Woman, why do you involve me? My hour has not yet come." —John 2:3–4

But Mary doesn't argue. She doesn't plead. She doesn't panic. She turns to the servants and says: "Do whatever He tells you."

That's not just maternal instinct. That's prophetic confidence.

Mary didn't demand a miracle. She simply made room for it. And Jesus turned water into wine—not to impress a crowd, but to honor a relationship built on trust.

Men, take note: that's what trusted leadership looks like. It's not about being the center of focus—it's about being the anchor when things feel like they're drifting. And when you lead from a place of conviction, not craving, you won't have to worry about repeating words or chasing moments. Your life will speak for itself.

When Trust Carries You

There's a certain kind of bond that needs no instructions.
The friend who hands you keys before you ask.
The mentor who sends a text right when doubt creeps in.
The father who doesn't say much, but you always felt covered.

- It's the older brother who checks in before you break down.
- It's the deacon who slips an envelope in your hand and says, "Just keep going."
- It's the friend who pulls you into prayer—not a podcast.

This isn't emotional fluff. This is manhood that moves. Brotherhood that builds. This is the kind of presence that strengthens a room without needing to speak in it.

And let's be real—it's rare. Because most of us were trained to speak our values, to prove our worth, and to assert our position. But the Word is clear:

> "Even a fool is thought wise if he keeps silent, and discerning if he holds his tongue."
> —Proverbs 17:28 (NIV)

Some of the wisest men don't talk much. They just carry truth in how they live. That's what it means to be trusted without a word.

When God Trusts You Without Words

Some of the most powerful moments in the Bible are when God doesn't explain Himself, but He still chooses someone.

- Noah builds an ark before rain exists.
- Joseph keeps his head down in prison before the dream ever comes true.
- Abraham climbs a mountain with his son—no instructions, no blueprint, just "Go."

These are men who walked without clarity, but walked anyway.

Being trusted by God isn't always exciting. Sometimes it's exhausting. Because He'll give you the assignment without an explanation, and He expects you to carry it—not because you understand, but because you're obedient.

When God trusts you without a word, it means you've proven that your "yes" doesn't require an audience. Your faith doesn't demand a forecast. And your loyalty doesn't shift with public opinion.

That's when legacy begins.

Legacy Built in Silence

Mary, Martha, and Jesus. Mary, Jesus, and the wine. The thread between them isn't just miracles—it's maturity. A trust that didn't need fanfare to be fruitful.

So, what does legacy look like in a man's life?
- It's sons who know how to cry without shame.
- It's daughters who say, "My dad didn't talk much, but he always showed up."
- It's brothers who trust you with their truth because they've seen your consistency.
- It's a home that doesn't crumble when storms hit, because the foundation was laid in faith, not flash.

Legacy isn't what you leave behind. It's what lives because you stayed.

And maybe that's the challenge for you—to be the man who listens more than he lectures. To be the brother who doesn't always need to be understood, but who's always reliable. A man others trust in rooms where words don't matter, but presence does.

You may not say much. But you carry much. You hold space. You build bridges. You speak life with your decisions, not just your declarations.

Because trust isn't built in what you preach—it's built in how you live.

And when it's all said and done, after the voices fade and the noise dies down, may it be found that you were a man trusted without a word.

A man like Lazarus, who Jesus wept over.
A man like Joseph, who God used in silence.
A man like you, still standing.
Quietly obedient.
Unshakably loyal.
Fully His.

CHAPTER 8

Tangled Threads of Fate

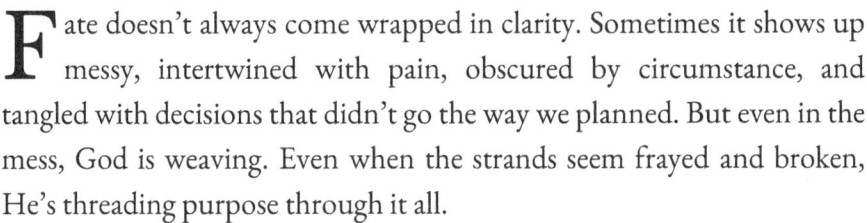

Fate doesn't always come wrapped in clarity. Sometimes it shows up messy, intertwined with pain, obscured by circumstance, and tangled with decisions that didn't go the way we planned. But even in the mess, God is weaving. Even when the strands seem frayed and broken, He's threading purpose through it all.

Your life isn't random. Your path isn't accidental. There's a tension you feel between where you started and where you're headed. That tension is the loom where destiny gets formed. *Tangled Threads of Fate* isn't just about the big moments that define you—it's about the quiet ones that shape you. The silent decisions. The hidden obedience. The private wrestling nobody sees but God.

God never promised a straight line. But He did promise a sovereign hand. He didn't say it would be simple. He didn't say we wouldn't face detours, delays, or disappointments.

But He did say, "I know the plans I have for you, plans to prosper you and not to harm you, plans to give you hope and a future." —Jeremiah 29:11

He didn't say you'd always understand. But He did say that if you trust Him, He'll make your path straight—even when you're walking through the crooked, the confusing, and the unclear.

"Trust in the Lord with all your heart and lean not on your own understanding; in all your ways acknowledge Him, and He shall direct your paths." —Proverbs 3:5–6

And when the threads of your life feel tangled beyond repair—when your story doesn't look like what you thought, and your journey seems too broken to matter—He reminds you:

"I will never leave you nor forsake you." —Hebrews 13:5
"All things work together for the good of those who love God and are called according to His purpose." —Romans 8:28

That's the promise.

Not that every thread will make sense right away. But that every thread is in His hand.
So no, you weren't promised a straight path.
But you *were* promised a faithful God.

When we deepen our relationship with God, we strengthen the threads that bind us to one another, and that's more than enough.

In this chapter, we're looking at two lives that seemed unlikely to be connected: Esther, a Jewish girl turned queen, and Paul, a Christian killer turned apostle. Different stories. Different backgrounds. But one truth: God was in the threadwork.

This is not a motivational metaphor. This is biblical. These stories were not fairy tales. They were forged in fear, loss, silence, courage, and calling. And if God could pull purpose out of their chaos, He can do the same with yours.

So don't despise the detours. Don't overlook the strange turns. Even when life knots up, the thread is still in His hand.

Esther: Positioned by Providence

Esther didn't ask for royalty. She didn't sign up for legacy. She was orphaned, raised by her cousin, and taken into the Persian palace as part of a king's beauty search. It didn't look like calling. It looked like captivity.

But God doesn't need a pulpit to set up purpose. There are moments when God places you inside something broken—not to blend in, but to bring change. Esther didn't ascend to royalty for comfort or crowns. Her position was a setup, not for status, but for salvation.

Beneath the layers of palace life—perfumes, protocols, and political games—God was forging a deliverer. Her heritage stayed hidden. Her power, quiet. But when the threat against her people surfaced, her silence couldn't stay. Purpose called. And obedience answered.

Her cousin Mordecai sent a message that shook the room:

"Who knows if perhaps you were made queen for just such a time as this?" —Esther 4:14, NLT

And Esther didn't shrink back. She didn't hide behind her crown. She stepped into destiny, even when it could've cost her life.

"I will go in to see the king. If I must die, I must die." —Esther 4:16, NLT

That's what courage looks like—when your faith speaks louder than your fear. When you realize your placement isn't about your comfort but your calling.

Esther fasted. Prayed. Planned. And then she moved. In a series of God-ordained moments, she exposed Haman, saved her people, and changed the course of history.

Brother, sometimes you're not in that job, that family, or that city to survive. You're there because someone's breakthrough is tied to your obedience—and sometimes, your own breakthrough is tied to it too.

Paul: From Persecutor to Preacher

But if anyone looked too far gone, it was Paul. Back when he was still Saul, he didn't just dislike Christians. He hunted them. Approved their execution. Carried religious authority like a sword.

But God doesn't choose the qualified—He qualifies the chosen.
And on the road to Damascus, everything changed.

"As he was approaching Damascus on this mission, a light from heaven suddenly shone down around him. He fell to the ground and heard a voice saying, 'Saul! Saul! Why are you persecuting me?'
'Who are you, lord?' Saul asked.
And the voice replied, 'I am Jesus, the one you are persecuting! Now get up and go into the city, and you will be told what you must do.'"
—Acts 9:3–6, NLT

That was the moment the tangled thread turned. Saul's reputation didn't stop Jesus. His record didn't disqualify him. His past didn't cancel his future.

"Go, for Saul is my chosen instrument to take my message to the Gentiles and to kings, as well as to the people of Israel."
—Acts 9:15, NLT

Paul's life didn't just shift—it exploded with purpose. The persecutor became a preacher. The destroyer became a disciple-maker. His letters would shape the Church for generations. What does that tell you?

It tells you no one is too far gone.
It tells you your failures don't get the final word.
It tells you God can take a tangled mess and use it to preach the Gospel to the nations.

Your Damascus moment might not come with lightning—but it will come with a choice. Will you let God redirect the thread?

Because here's the truth: God doesn't waste what He redeems. He doesn't salvage your past to sit it on a shelf. He uses it. He sends it. He threads it into someone else's healing.

That shame you thought disqualified you? God turns it into wisdom. That regret that used to carry you? He recycles it into testimony.

The same man who once dragged believers out of their homes would later write from a prison cell about the freedom we have in Christ.

That's the God we serve. He doesn't just restore—He repurposes.

And maybe, just maybe, the very things you've tried to bury are the same things He wants to use. Not to humiliate you, but to help someone else. Not to reopen wounds, but to reveal grace.

What if your story, like Paul's, is the key to someone else's freedom?

So don't rush to untangle the thread. Let Him weave it. Let Him shape it. Because the same God who met Paul on the road is walking yours too. Not to condemn you, but to commission you. Not to erase your history, but to give it eternal meaning.

You're not just being redirected—you're being redefined.

Destiny, Detours, and Divine Timing

Esther didn't know her crown would save a nation. Paul didn't know his detour would build the Church. You won't always see the pattern. But you can trust the process. The lives of Esther and Paul remind us that God is not random. He is a Weaver. And He knows how to pull glory out of what looks like ruin.

They didn't have all the answers. But they leaned into the thread anyway. They stayed faithful to the hand holding it, even when the picture wasn't clear.

> "And we know that in all things God works for the good of those who love him, who have been called according to his purpose."
> —Romans 8:28, NIV

It's not always clean. It's not always quick. But it's always connected. God is not wasting any part of your journey. Not the mistakes. Not the delays. Not the pain.

> "Faith shows the reality of what we hope for; it is the evidence of things we cannot see."
> —Hebrews 11:1, NLT

It is through the lives of Esther and Paul that we are given a glimpse into the mysterious yet purposeful ways God orchestrates the course of history. Their stories challenge us to live with purpose, faith, and a deep awareness of our part in the divine tapestry of life, trusting that even the most tangled threads can be woven into a masterpiece of God's design if we trust and believe that He is able.

What This Means for You, Brother

You may feel like your thread is too tangled—too many wrong turns, too many missed moments, too much silence from heaven.

But the same God who called Esther from silence and Paul from violence is still calling men like you today.

Men who don't need all the answers, but are willing to say yes anyway.
Men who will step into the room when fear says hide.
Men who will preach with their lives when the world tries to cancel their voice.

You're not just living your story. You're walking out a page in His.

You may not wear a crown. You may not write epistles. But your "yes" still matters. Your obedience still echoes. Your life, no matter how tangled, can still preach purpose.

So take courage. Keep walking. Keep trusting the hand that holds your thread.

Because the tangled thread in your hand... it's in God's loom.

Let it be said of you: he didn't need the full picture to move forward. He trusted the Weaver. He stayed when it was hard. He believed when it didn't make sense. And in the end, his thread was part of the masterpiece God had in mind all along.

You're not just part of the story, brother.
You're part of the threadwork of eternity.

CHAPTERS 9
Two Halves of a Whole

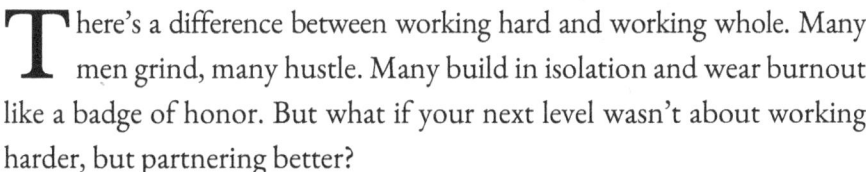

There's a difference between working hard and working whole. Many men grind, many hustle. Many build in isolation and wear burnout like a badge of honor. But what if your next level wasn't about working harder, but partnering better?

Two Halves of a Whole is about the power of partnership. It's about recognizing that even the strongest men weren't made to go at it alone. In fact, in the Kingdom, we were never meant to.

From the very beginning, God declared, "It is not good for man to be alone." —Genesis 2:18

That wasn't just about marriage; it was about mission. About ministry. About movement. One man can make noise. But two can move mountains.

Everywhere you look in life, the most meaningful impact happens when two or more people come together under a shared purpose and mutual submission.

There's the husband and wife, whose union reflects the image of Christ and the Church, built not just on love, but on sacrificial teamwork and spiritual alignment.

There's the business partner who sees the vision you carry and brings strategy, accountability, and shared risk to make it a reality.

There's the ministry leader and armor-bearer, where one casts vision and the other carries weight, both honoring the call by serving each other.

There's the mentor and mentee, where wisdom and hunger collide, and the lessons of one generation are passed to the next.

There's the brother and friend, walking shoulder to shoulder, not just sharing life, but sharpening each other for the battle.

There are the teacher and student, the coach and athlete, the pastor and deacon, and the visionary and executor—partnerships that work not because both are the same but because both bring something essential to the table.

In the Kingdom, we don't compete, we complete. And when we walk in unity, the mission multiplies.

We live in a culture that glorifies self-made success. Lone wolves. Solo kings. But the Kingdom was never designed to be built by individuals. It was built by brothers. By partnerships. By co-laborers in Christ. Because no matter how gifted you are, if you're only operating in isolation, you're only giving half the picture. You're only bringing half the strength. You're only doing half the work.
And half doesn't make whole.

Priscilla and Aquila: Unity in Action

In Acts 18:2–3, we're introduced to Priscilla and Aquila, a married couple who were tentmakers by trade but kingdom-builders by calling. When Paul arrives in Corinth, he meets them and stays with them, working alongside them in both profession and purpose.

Later, in Acts 18:26, this same couple pulls aside Apollos, a passionate but incomplete preacher, and together, they teach him the way of God more accurately. They weren't flashy. They weren't fighting for the spotlight. They were just faithful.

What's powerful here isn't just that Priscilla and Aquila did ministry; it's that they did it together. They moved in sync, taught in unity, and covered each other's blind spots. That's what partnership looks like in the Kingdom: two halves bringing their full selves to a shared mission.

For the modern man, this matters. Whether in your marriage, your ministry, or your brotherhood, your strength doesn't diminish when you share the work. It multiplies. You don't lose identity in partnership. You sharpen it.

Too many men live like they've got something to prove. Like receiving help is a weakness. But if the Apostle Paul could build tents with Aquila and teach the Word with Priscilla, you can link arms with someone too.

You don't need to be the only name on the flyer. You need to be the kind of man who's effective in the field.

Paul and Barnabas: When Partnership Fuels Purpose

Acts 13:2–3 gives us another powerful image of partnership, this time in the launch of Paul and Barnabas. The Holy Spirit says, "Set apart for me Barnabas and Saul for the work to which I have called them." Two men. One mission. A world to reach.

Their unity was so strong that Scripture describes it as God Himself choosing them for the assignment. They traveled, preached, suffered, built churches, and pushed the Gospel into new territory. Their partnership didn't dilute their power; it released it.

Yet even they had a conflict (Acts 15:36–40). Their sharp disagreement over John Mark caused them to part ways. And here's the lesson: not all partnerships are perfect. But that doesn't mean they weren't purposeful.

In life, you may work with brothers who challenge you. You may disagree. That doesn't disqualify the mission. It reminds you that grace, forgiveness, and maturity are essential to Kingdom work. Because at the end of the day, this isn't about your ego, it's about God's glory.

What Half Really Looks Like

Have you ever tried to carry a couch by yourself?
It's not just heavy, it's awkward. It leans. It drags. It scratches the floor. That's what doing Kingdom work alone looks like. You might get the job done, but it's crooked, messy, and painful.

Now imagine someone on the other side, lifting with you, adjusting the angle, and walking in rhythm. Suddenly, the same load feels lighter. That's not just physics. That's partnership.

Half looks like a father trying to raise sons with no spiritual support. Like a leader running a ministry with no accountability. Like a man pursuing purpose without wise counsel. And half, no matter how strong it is, still leaves you vulnerable.

Jesus sent His disciples out two-by-two. Not because He lacked laborers, but because He knew the power of partnership. He said, "For where two or three gather in my name, there am I with them" (Matthew 18:20). When unity shows up, so does He.

So who's on the other end of your mission?

Moses and Hur: When You Need Someone to Hold Your Arms

In Exodus 17:11–12, Israel is at war with Amalek. As long as Moses holds up his hands, Israel wins. But when his arms grow tired, they begin to lose. So Aaron and Hur come alongside him—not to take the rod, but to hold his arms up.

Moses had the authority. But without support, even authority grows weak. Let that sink in.

You may be the head of the house, the leader in your church, the visionary in your business, but if no one's holding up your arms, your strength won't last. God designed the work to be shared not just in responsibility, but in endurance.

You don't need men to carry you. But you do need men to lift you.

Joshua and Caleb: Brothers in Belief

When the twelve spies came back from scouting the Promised Land in Numbers 13-14, only Joshua and Caleb came with faith. The others saw giants. These two saw victory.

Sometimes, partnership isn't about shared skills, it's about shared spirit.

They weren't the loudest, but they stood in belief. They backed each other up. They didn't flinch under pressure. And because of their unity, God preserved them to enter the land.

Brother, who do you believe in? Who fuels your faith instead of feeding your fear? Who speaks life when others speak doubt?

A partnership doesn't just help you carry the work. It enables you to carry the weight of faith.

When Co-Laboring Becomes Kingdom Building

Imagine a construction site where every builder refuses to share tools. No one talks. No one measures twice. Everyone builds their own corner in their own way.

What happens?

The structure collapses. Not because they didn't work, but because they didn't work together.

That's the danger of Kingdom men building without unity. Ministries crumble. Vision loses impact. The wall Nehemiah rebuilt in 52 days? It took families stationed side-by-side. That's how Kingdom walls go up. Shoulder to shoulder. One hand on the sword. One on the work.

We're not here to outshine each other. We're here to outbuild the enemy.

The Danger of Hoarding the Mission

When men hoard the call, the church hurts. When men compete instead of collaborating, souls lose. When we chase platforms instead of people, the mission gets delayed.

We are not building empires. We are building the Body. And no part of the body can survive cut off from the rest.

Your gift is not meant to isolate you. It's intended to integrate you. The moment you start believing you're the only one who can do it, you're no longer building for God. You're building for yourself. And that will always crumble.

Two Halves, One Whole, One Purpose

Partnership requires humility. It means asking for help, offering help, and celebrating someone else's strength without feeling insecure about your own. It means believing that God gets more glory when we move together than when we stand alone.

Jesus sent His disciples into the world not as solo warriors, but as unified laborers. He prayed in John 17: "That they may be one as we are one." That's the heart of the Gospel. Not just individual salvation, but collective transformation.

Brother, if you're holding half, find someone to complete the other—not to complete you, but to complete the mission. Because two halves of a whole don't just get more done.

They look more like Jesus.

CHAPTER 10
Silent Sacrifices

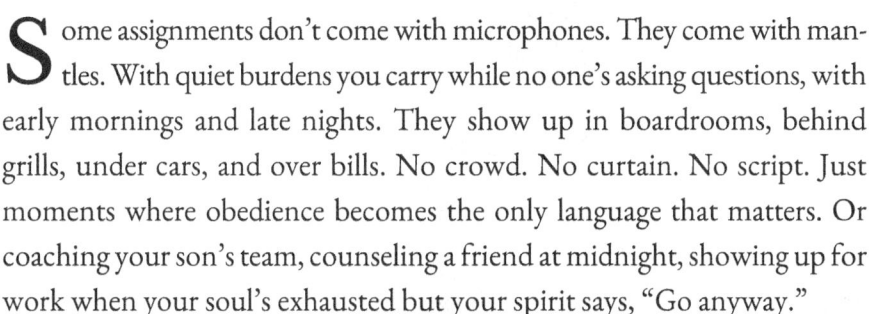

Some assignments don't come with microphones. They come with mantles. With quiet burdens you carry while no one's asking questions, with early mornings and late nights. They show up in boardrooms, behind grills, under cars, and over bills. No crowd. No curtain. No script. Just moments where obedience becomes the only language that matters. Or coaching your son's team, counseling a friend at midnight, showing up for work when your soul's exhausted but your spirit says, "Go anyway."

This kind of calling doesn't raise its voice, it raises your standard. It teaches you that purpose isn't always loud, but it's always weighty. It's the discipline to stay faithful when everything in you wants to fold. It's showing up with consistency when convenience would be easier. It's laying down your preferences for someone else's peace. Not because it's flashy, but because it's right.

This is the kind of sacrifice that doesn't make headlines but makes heaven lean in. The kind of quiet strength that shifts families, generations, and spiritual atmospheres—not through performance, but through posture. In the Kingdom, what's done in secret often carries more power than what's done in public. Because real sacrifice—God-honoring, Christlike, soul-wrenching sacrifice—isn't always loud. Sometimes, it's just obedience in the dark.

"But when you give to someone in need, don't let your left hand know what your right hand is doing. Give your gifts in private, and your Father, who sees everything, will reward you." Matthew 6:3–4 (NLT)

This chapter isn't about what people see. It's about what God honors. These are the sacrifices that build altars in the unseen. The ones that forge a legacy. The ones that cost something private but yield something powerful.

Because the truth is, God doesn't need an echo to respond. He moves at the sound of obedience.

It's about men who get low so someone else can rise. Men who pour out without applause. Men who serve quietly, pray deeply, give faithfully, and bleed spiritually—and never post about it. Because they're not chasing credit. They're choosing the altar.

When Silence Is Strength

The governor's room was cold with tension. Pilate stared Jesus down, confused, frustrated, maybe even afraid. He was Rome's authority in Jerusalem. But at that moment, he was the one looking for answers.

"Where are You from?" he asked.

No reply.

Not a word. No explanation. No defense. No breakdown of the prophecy being fulfilled. Just silence.

"He took Jesus back into the headquarters again and asked him, 'Where are you from?' But Jesus gave no answer." John 19:9

Men, there's a kind of silence that speaks louder than shouting. A silence that doesn't mean passivity; it means power under control. This wasn't the silence of confusion or weakness. This was the stillness of a Savior who knew the assignment. Jesus didn't need to validate Himself to a man on a temporary throne. He was answering to the throne that had no end.

And neither do you.

There will be moments in life where your manhood will be questioned, your integrity tested, and your name dragged. You'll be tempted to clap back to prove your worth, to fight fire with fire. But hear this: not every fight is yours to fight. And not every critic deserves your energy.

Jesus stood in power, not because He said a lot, but because He said what mattered... when it mattered. His restraint was warfare. His silence was strategy.

Some of the greatest moments of your manhood won't be seen in how loudly you lead, but in how quietly you surrender. Not to people—but to purpose.

Choosing not to respond is not cowardice, it's courage. It's emotional discipline. It's trusting that God will speak for you in rooms you refuse to fight in. And for some of you, that's the next level of growth. You're not in a season of silence because you've lost your voice. You're in it because God is teaching you to hear His. You're learning that your strength doesn't come from being understood; it comes from being obedient.

So the next time someone questions your calling... pause. You don't have to explain a word. Let your posture answer for you. Let your fruit speak for you. Let your peace confuse them. And let your Father vindicate you.

Because when you know who you are—and more importantly, whose you are—you don't need to shout. You just stand.

Stephen: Forgiveness in the Fire

As rocks rained down, Stephen didn't curse the crowd. He didn't beg for rescue. He didn't hold a grudge. He stood in the gap between heaven and earth, bloodied but bold, and he released forgiveness that mirrored his Savior.

"Then he fell on his knees and cried out, 'Lord, do not hold this sin against them.' When he had said this, he fell asleep." Acts 7:60

This wasn't a preacher looking for a platform. It was a servant refusing to let pain silence his purpose. Stephen's final words weren't about revenge; they were about redemption. His death became a seed, and Saul of Tarsus, who stood watching, would later become Paul the Apostle. Never underestimate the power of obedience in the fire.

Men, sometimes the person watching your suffering will be the one changed by it. The very moment you feel forsaken might become the moment someone else's faith is born. And that's the tension of sacrifice: you bleed while they breathe. You die to self while someone else wakes up to destiny.

When Silence Speaks Louder Than Words

Silent sacrifice doesn't mean weakness; it means wisdom. It means choosing when to speak and when to stay still. It's the discipline of restraint when you're misjudged, misunderstood, or mistreated. Choosing not to broadcast every good deed. Choosing to cover your brother instead of exposing his mistake. Choosing to pray when you'd rather post. Choosing to worship when no one is watching.

"Be on your guard; stand firm in the faith; be courageous; be strong. Do everything in love." 1 Corinthians 16:13–14 (NIV)

It's what you carry when decisions aren't yours to make, but responsibility still finds its way to your hands. When no one's asking your opinion, but everything still leans on your faithfulness. When you're in the background, but your spirit is in full obedience.

This is where spiritual warfare lives—not just in the public declaration, but in the private decision.

- It's a man driving his sick mother to the hospital every day, and never missing a Sunday to serve.
- It's a father turning down a promotion to be present for his children.

- It's a pastor who preaches to ten people with the same fire he'd bring to a thousand.
- It's the friend who prays for his brother behind closed doors and never tells a soul.

These sacrifices don't go viral. But they break chains. They summon angels. They shift the atmosphere. Because what goes unnoticed by man is often honored by God, and what's overlooked on earth can be celebrated in heaven.

The Fire Meets the Offering

The altar isn't glamorous; it's gritty. It's the place where pride dies, control surrenders, and obedience becomes the offering. It's not where men go to get noticed—it's where they go to be refined. It's where something gets laid down so that something greater can rise.

You won't find filters at the altar. No fancy backdrops. No curated image. Just a man, his God, and a "yes" that costs something. Ambition craves a platform. But the anointing comes where the fire falls, and fire doesn't fall on performances. It falls on sacrifice. When you choose the altar, you decide to surrender over status. You choose to be emptied so God can fill you. You desire refinement over recognition. It's not about less visibility; it's about more intimacy.

That's the place where God meets man. That's where He turns ashes into beauty.

Take Elijah, for example—not the chariot-riding prophet, but the altar-building servant. On Mount Carmel, Elijah didn't build a platform to prove anything. He rebuilt an altar to restore something. While the prophets of Baal danced and shouted for hours, Elijah poured water on the offering and simply prayed (1 Kings 18:36–38). No theatrics. Just trust.

And what happened? The fire of the Lord fell. Not on the noise. Not on the crowd. But on the obedience.

God didn't respond to drama. He responded to surrender.

This is the fire God still responds to—the man who quietly rebuilds what others let fall apart. The man who kneels when others perform. The man who says, "Not my will, but Your will be done." Luke 22:42

That's where legacy is forged. That's where God answers by fire.

Choosing the Long Obedience

Obedience rarely feels glamorous. It doesn't always come with spiritual goosebumps. Sometimes, it's just staying married when it would be easier to walk away. Sometimes, it's paying your tithes when the bills don't add up. Sometimes, it's sticking with a struggling brother when everyone else has left. Sometimes, it's not quitting—just because you're tired.

Obedience isn't a moment; it's a muscle. And every time you say "yes" to God when no one sees it, you're strengthening it.

Brother, your silent obedience might be the most prophetic thing you ever do. Because what you do in silence becomes the soundtrack of someone else's salvation. And while the world claps for the loud, heaven crowns the faithful.

The Call to Lay It Down

Jesus said in Luke 9:23, "Whoever wants to be my disciple must deny themselves and take up their cross daily and follow me."

Silent sacrifice is daily. It's repeated. It's sometimes lonely. But it's always worth it. Maybe your cross isn't visible, but it's heavy. Perhaps it's the burden to stay when others have left. To forgive when others hold grudges. To give when you barely have enough. To fight for people who stopped fighting for themselves.

Whatever it is, don't drop it. Please don't run from it. Lay it down. Daily. Again and again. Because that cross—*that silent weight*—is shaping you into someone the devil can't move.

Let it be said of you, not that you ran toward approval, but that you walked with Jesus toward the cross. That when others looked for recognition, you looked for the altar. That when it cost you something, you didn't flinch. You laid down your pride. You laid down your comfort. You laid down your life so someone else could stand. But I pray you don't have to do that literally—Jesus already did. It's a metaphor for laying down ego, control, and convenience so someone else can rise, heal, breathe, and walk forward in strength.

Let it be said of you that you stood in the middle, not for credit, but for your brother. That when the battle came to your doorstep, your family, or your church, you didn't fold. You fasted. You interceded. You led with prayer and perseverance, even when your own strength was running low. You showed up with consistency, protected what mattered, and trusted God to carry the rest.

Jesus isn't looking for performers; He's looking for partners. For He is the King of kings and the Lord of lords, and we are to be kings in our own right—ruling with righteousness, leading with humility, and sacrificing with purpose.

He's calling men who will share in His burden, not just His benefits. Men who pick up spiritual weight, not for applause, but because they know eternity is heavy. Men who don't just speak about sacrifice but live it—in their decisions, in prayer, in discipline, in love.

So brother, build the altar. Offer the sacrifice. Even if it's quiet. Even if it costs you. Even if it goes unspoken in rooms full of noise.

Because silent sacrifice still shakes hell. And God never forgets what's placed in His hands.

"Your Father, who sees what is done in secret, will reward you." Matthew 6:4

CHAPTER 11
Built to Lead: The Call of the Older Man

There's a reason Paul didn't just write to the crowd—he wrote to the pillars. To the men who'd weathered storms, buried brothers, built families, made mistakes, and kept going. Paul told Titus to speak directly to the older men. Not as a side note. Not as an afterthought. But as a foundation.

Why?

Because older men carry something the next generation desperately needs, but rarely asks for.

Not just wisdom, but weight.

Not just memories, but momentum.

Not just "back in my day" stories, but evidence of what it looks like to live through failure, get back up, and still follow Jesus.

"Though the righteous fall seven times, they rise again." Proverbs 24:16a

These are the men who've survived the silence. Who've raised families without applause, served the church without a platform, and carried the quiet burdens of life that only a few ever notice.

They've seen enough to speak about what matters, and lived long enough to know what doesn't. And yet, in many churches, they're ignored and left on the sidelines—treated like their time is past, when biblically, their time is more important than ever.

Because what good is it for younger men to run fast if they have no one to help them run well?
What good is energy without guidance?
Passion without perspective?

We don't need more opinions—we need more examples. Older men who don't just remember the fire but still carry the flame. Men who don't shout about the way things used to be, but live like the Kingdom still has work to do.

This generation doesn't just need fathers; it needs finishers. Men who model what it means to grow older without growing colder. To age without quitting. To be seasoned without being silent.

That's why Titus was told to speak directly. Clearly. Boldly.

Because this assignment isn't casual—it's critical. The future health of the church depends on it. The strength of the next generation depends on it. And the unity of brotherhood requires it.

Titus 2 doesn't waste words. It gives a clear blueprint. And it begins with a charge:

"Teach the older men to be temperate, worthy of respect, self-controlled, and sound in faith, in love and in endurance." Titus 2:2

This isn't a sentimental nod to the elders. It's a divine assignment. A call to character. A mandate to be men of depth, not just age. Older men aren't just survivors of time—they're meant to be stewards of truth. Custodians of character. Brothers who've walked through fire and come out with something worth passing on.

This is about more than just aging. It's about legacy. Leadership. Brotherhood. Because the younger ones—they're watching. Listening. Deciding who they'll become based on how you live now.

And the church? It can't be built on trends. It's built on the backs of trustworthy men. Men who know who they are. Who aren't tossed by emotion or ego. Who don't just quote Scripture, but embody it.

Let's break it down.

Temperate: Balanced in the Battle

To be temperate means to be even-keeled. Steady. Sober-minded. You don't fly off the handle. You don't get drunk on power, rage, or nostalgia. You know how to hold the line without losing your mind.

This doesn't mean you're passive. It means you're anchored. And in a world full of volatility, that makes you dangerous—in the right way.

Temperate men create safe spaces. Their presence speaks peace. Their silence settles chaos. Their counsel doesn't just come from books; it comes from battle scars.

You've lived long enough to know that not everything deserves your reaction. Not every argument is worth the energy. That some battles are better fought on your knees than with your fists.

So when God calls older men to be temperate, He's not calling you to check out. He's calling you to be the thermostat, not the thermometer. Set the temperature. Don't just reflect the heat—regulate it.

Worthy of Respect: Not Just Aged, but Anchored

Respect isn't something you demand. It's something you walk in.

To be worthy of respect means your life holds weight—not because you're perfect, but because you're consistent. People trust your "yes" and your "no." You don't speak on everything, but when you do, it matters.

You've earned the right to speak not by volume, but by virtue. You've carried burdens, paid prices, and still kept your integrity intact. And that speaks louder than titles or platforms ever could.

This isn't about being honored—it's about being honorable. It's about how you treat your wife and how you love your children, how you speak to the young men in the back who don't know how to tie a tie but want to learn how to pray.

Because a man who's worthy of respect doesn't just build a name—he builds people.

Self-Controlled: The Fruit of Spiritual Maturity

There are things older men shouldn't still be wrestling with. Not because you've mastered life, but because you've matured in Christ.

Self-control is the ability to say "no" when everything in you wants to say "yes." It's not just about lust or addiction—it's about stewardship. How you spend your time. What you entertain. How you respond when you're challenged.

A self-controlled man doesn't let feelings drive the wheel. He lets faith take the lead.

And in a generation driven by impulse, we need examples of what it means to slow down, think through, and act in step with the Spirit.

This is where the younger men need you—not to shout at them, but to show them. To say, "I've been where you are. And here's how I kept my soul anchored."

Sound in Faith, Love, and Endurance

Paul didn't stop at behavior. He drilled deeper—into the inner life.

Sound in faith means you're not tossed around by trends or new doctrines. You don't need gimmicks or applause to stay steady. You know who Jesus is, and you trust Him when it's easy—and especially when it's not.

Sound in love means you don't grow bitter with age—you grow better. You don't just tolerate people—you pour into them. You love with action, not just talk. You forgive, you mentor, you embrace, you show up.

Sound in endurance means you haven't quit, even when you could've. Your knees might ache, but your spirit still runs. You've learned that consistency outlasts charisma. That God honors the man who endures. Not the loudest one, but the one who's faithful.

A Brother's Keeper at Every Stage

This is where Titus 2 connects directly to the call of brotherhood.

Older men, this world needs your voice, your walk, your wisdom. Not just for nostalgia's sake, but for survival. The younger generation is under fire. And they're not looking for influencers—they're looking for intercessors.

They need men who will:

- Pray for them.
- Walk with them.
- Correct them with love.
- Speak life when they want to quit.
- Model Christ when they're tempted to compromise.

Brotherhood doesn't retire. You don't age out of it.

Men leave church, stop serving, quit jobs, leave people, because it's their choice, and sometimes just because. But you don't age out of accountability. You deepen into it.

Scripture reminds us in **Psalm 92:14 (NKJV):** *"They shall still bear fruit in old age; They shall be fresh and flourishing."*

That means if you're still breathing, you're still bearing. If you're still here, God's still expecting fruit.

You don't graduate from being a keeper, you grow into it. A seasoned man of God doesn't fade into the background. He steps forward with stability so younger men can lean in. His presence should bring order to chaos. His words should carry a lifetime of lessons. His faithfulness becomes a refuge when the world gets shaky.

It's like a grandfather who never says much at the dinner table, but when he speaks, everyone listens. Not because he's loud, but because his life has proven he's worth hearing. That's the kind of weight older brothers are meant to carry.

Not dominance, but depth. Not control, but credibility.

So don't disqualify yourself because you've aged. That may be the very reason God's calling you now.

Legacy Looks Like You

You don't need a mic to mentor. You don't need a spotlight to have influence. You need to be faithful with what God has placed in your hands. Because somewhere, a young man is watching. Listening. Deciding.
What he sees in you will help shape what he becomes. Not because you're flawless, but because you're real. You've stayed in the fight. You've repented when you got it wrong. You've kept walking.
"Follow my example, as I follow the example of Christ."
1 Corinthians 11:1

And that, brother, is legacy.

Final Words: Built to Lead

That's why being a brother's keeper isn't just for the young, it's the responsibility of the seasoned. And your life is the sermon that many of these men will never hear from a pulpit, but will remember forever. This world doesn't just need younger men on fire. It needs older men who've stayed faithful. Who still believe. Who still love. Who still pour out.

"They will still bear fruit in old age, they will stay fresh and green...", **Psalm 92:14**

You are not retired, you're required. God has not sidelined you, He's sent you.

So rise up, builder of men. Brother of many. Keeper of the next generation.

You're not just older. You're built to lead.

CHAPTER 12

Legacy of Love and Loss

Every man leaves something behind. Whether it's a name, a reputation, a scar, or a seed, your life echoes after you. And what you do with your faith, your trials, your relationships, and your choices will either build something eternal or bury something sacred.

"The world and its desires pass away, but whoever does the will of God lives forever." 1 John 2:17

This isn't just the end of a book. It's the beginning of a new chapter in your legacy. Because everything we've unpacked—being your brother's keeper, choosing loyalty, walking in partnership, trusting silently, serving sacrificially—it all comes down to one defining question:

What will outlive you?

In a world obsessed with leaving your mark, the Kingdom calls for men to leave something much greater: a legacy.
Not one built on applause, but on faith.
Not one crafted in comfort, but carved out through love and loss.

Through the kind of love that shows up when it's inconvenient. The kind that doesn't just speak the truth, it walks it out. The kind that forgives without being asked. That sacrifices without being recognized. That covers without keeping score.

It's the love a man carries for his brother—a love that keeps showing up for the people of God, even when you're tired, even when you feel overlooked, even when it would be easier to quit.

It's the kind of love that reflects the Father—steady, strong, and unshakable. The type of love that forgives without being asked, that fights for family when it's fractured, that stays loyal even after trust has been tested.

And loss—the kind that leaves you breathless. The type that empties rooms, shatters plans, and leaves prayers hanging in the air. Loss of people, seasons, dreams, and even pieces of yourself. But instead of shutting you down, it opens you up to what really matters.

"Praise be to the God and Father of our Lord Jesus Christ, the Father of compassion and the God of all comfort, who comforts us in all our troubles, so that we can comfort those in any trouble with the comfort we ourselves receive from God." 2 Corinthians 1:3–4

Because legacy isn't built in the absence of pain—it's born in the middle of it.

Love shapes the heart.
Loss reveals its depth.
And legacy is formed where the two collide—where sacrifice fuels compassion, where grief becomes fuel for grace, and where your scars don't disqualify you, they mark you as a man who's still standing.
Still loving.
Still believing.
Still lifting others.
Still guarding the faith.
Still growing.
Still walking with integrity.

Still sowing seed when no one else is planting.
Still building bridges when others burn them.
Still moving toward the mark of the higher calling in Christ Jesus.
Still becoming the man God had in mind when He called you a "keeper."

This is how legacies are made. Not just in what we say, but in how we love. In how we endure. And how we lead when no one is watching but Heaven.

Job: Faith That Outlives the Fire

Job didn't just suffer loss—he lived through it. Family. Fortune. Health. Reputation. He lost what most men fear losing. And yet, he never lost his grasp on the One who mattered most.

"At this, Job got up and tore his robe and shaved his head. Then he fell to the ground in worship and said: 'Naked I came from my mother's womb, and naked I will depart. The Lord gave and the Lord has taken away; may the name of the Lord be praised.'" Job 1:20–21

That wasn't denial. That was devotion.

Job's pain wasn't poetic. It was real. And so is yours. Some of you know what it feels like to lose—not just things, but people, years, opportunities. To watch what you built collapse in a moment.

But what made Job a man of legacy wasn't that he avoided loss. It's that he remained faithful through it.

His worship wasn't a performance. It was a posture.
His endurance wasn't natural. It was supernatural.
And his story isn't a fairy tale—it's a blueprint.

A man with raw wounds and real questions, who chose to honor God even when Heaven went quiet.

This is the kind of faith that outlives the fire.

That plants something eternal in the ashes.

That passes something down to your sons, your brothers, and the next man watching how you respond when life doesn't make sense.

Paul: A Life Poured Out

Job teaches us how to suffer well. Paul teaches us how to finish strong.

"Five times I received from the Jews the forty lashes minus one. Three times I was beaten with rods, once I was pelted with stones, three times I was shipwrecked... I have been in danger from rivers, from bandits, from my fellow Jews... I have labored and toiled and have often gone without sleep; I have known hunger and thirst... and besides everything else, I face daily the pressure of my concern for all the churches." 2 Corinthians 11:24–28

Paul lost more than comfort. He lost friends. He lost freedom. He lost his reputation. And yet, he gave more than he ever lost. Because every wound he carried became a window for the Gospel. Paul didn't live to protect himself, he lived to pour himself out. He fought for the Church. He discipled younger men. He encouraged broken believers. He walked into hostile cities with nothing but the name of Jesus and the power of the Spirit.

And at the end of his life, he didn't ask for pity. He said this:

"I have fought the good fight, I have finished the race, I have kept the faith." 2 Timothy 4:7

That's legacy. That's the kind of man we're called to be. Not just one who talks a good game, but one who bleeds for the right cause.

The Brotherhood We Lose When We Don't Keep It

Some legacies aren't just built, they're broken. Because when we fail to keep our brothers, we don't just lose relationships, we lose spiritual inheritance. We lose the healing that happens in community. We lose the strength that multiplies when men walk together.

Cain's question still echoes: "Am I my brother's keeper?" And too many men are still answering: "No."

But when you abandon your brother, you don't just lose him. You lose part of yourself. You forfeit accountability. You disconnect from the Body. And you stop the flow of generational blessing that happens when men walk in unity, power, and authority. Every man you ignore is a legacy you diminish. Every brother you withhold forgiveness from is a future miracle you risk aborting.

We don't just mourn when we lose a brother to death, we grieve when we lose him to pride. To isolation. To addiction. To silence.

But it's not too late to change that.

Part of your legacy isn't just what you build, it's who you bring with you. It's the brother you refused to give up on. The co-worker you kept inviting. The young man you chose to disciple instead of just correct. That kind of legacy doesn't end with your death, it multiplies through the lives of others.

Don't let another generation of men grow up never hearing the truth from another man. Don't let silence win. Don't let shame have the last word. You carry light. You carry testimony. You carry the power to plant a seed that the Spirit of God can water and grow.

Be a man who wins souls, not just arguments. Be a man who sees the broken, and stays long enough to walk them toward wholeness. Because what good is your faith if you don't pass it on?

The Legacy of Love

Legacy isn't a monument, it's a movement. It's the decision to live for something beyond your own name. To love people deeply. To fight for what's right. To build bridges instead of burning them. To make room at your table. To carry the next man's burden when he can't lift his own.

The legacy of love is not soft, it's strong. It's what made Jesus lay His life down for His friends. It's what made Jesus leave Heaven—perfect, sinless—and step into a broken, messy world wrapped in flesh. He didn't come with an entourage. He came with intention. He walked among fishermen and tax collectors, sat with the rejected, touched the diseased, and dined with the despised. He called the unqualified. He calmed storms and confronted demons—not for show, but for souls. He didn't avoid the hard places; He walked straight into them.

"Whoever claims to live in him must live as Jesus did." 1 John 2:6

It's what made Him bend down and wash the dirt off His disciples' feet—even knowing one would betray Him, one would deny Him, and the rest would abandon Him. It's what made Him welcome the woman at the well, defend the woman caught in adultery, and weep with Mary and Martha at the tomb of Lazarus. It's what made Him choose a criminal's cross instead of a crown, and bleed for the very ones who shouted, "Crucify Him."

This kind of love wasn't passive. It was power under control. It was compassion laced with conviction. That's the model we follow. That's the legacy we carry.

It's what made Job pray for those who judged him. It's what made Paul mentor men even after they abandoned him.

And it's what will make you unshakable, unmovable, unstoppable.

The only way to become a man who can't be moved is to walk through moments that shake everything you thought you needed.

Sometimes a loss isn't a setback. It's a setup. It's how God clears the path to what actually matters. Some losses don't leave you empty, they free you. Losing your pride makes room for humility. Losing your ego makes space for wisdom. Losing your fear of failure makes space for faith. And losing your grip on what God never told you to carry? That's not a breakdown. That's a breakthrough.

These aren't just personal losses. They're spiritual shifts. You stop chasing what fades and start becoming a man who endures. You stop performing, and start transforming. And when you finally lose yourself in Christ, you're not left hollow, you're made whole.

"For you died to this life, and your real life is hidden with Christ in God." Colossians 3:3

That's not a weakness. That's where your real name gets spoken. That's where your legacy begins.

But the greatest loss? Is a man who refuses to give his life to something that matters. A man who sits on the sidelines while others bleed for the Gospel. A man who never fights for his brother. He never bows his head. He never lifts his hands. Never carries the fire.

Don't let that be you.

The Final Charge

Brother, the pages of your life are still being written. And everything you've read—every chapter, every truth, every challenge—isn't just theory. It's your call to action.

You're not too far behind to leave something lasting.
You're not too holy to grow deeper, serve harder, love wider, or pray with more power.
You're not too broken to build something meaningful.
You're not too small to shift something generational.
And you're definitely not too big to lose your fruit trying to protect your ego.

Humility is still the measure.
Faith is still the foundation.

Fruit is still the evidence.

So the question still stands:

What will your legacy be?

Will it be brotherhood that restores men who've fallen?
Will it be the connection that reminds someone they're not alone in the fight?
Will it be a community that builds bridges, breaks cycles, and binds up what the world tried to tear apart?
Will it be a unity that silences division?
Will it be truth wrapped in love, conviction anchored in compassion, and strength that doesn't flex, but lifts?

Brother, your legacy isn't just about what you build for yourself.
It's about who you build with, who you pour into, and what you leave behind for your bloodline.

It's about the man you choose to forgive when resentment feels justified. The brother you check in on when his silence speaks louder than his words.
It's the children you raise, the father you honor, the team you guide, the church you serve, the neighbor you protect, and the purpose you refuse to neglect.

Legacy is when your presence becomes someone else's stability,
when your discipline becomes someone else's breakthrough,
when your consistency becomes someone else's foundation.

Because love leaves fruit.
Loss builds roots.
And brotherhood leaves a trail.

Let it not just be a memory, but a movement.

Legacy isn't built in one big moment; it's built in daily decisions.

And this is yours.

Stand up.
Hold the line.
Carry your brother.
Finish well.

Because the story isn't over.
The Keeper is still keeping.
And the King is still calling.

ABOUT THE AUTHOR

Tony Austin Jr. is an author, preacher, teacher, and mentor whose mission is to help people discover their God-given identity and walk fully in purpose. As Executive Pastor of TBC Miami, Tony blends authenticity, humor, and practical wisdom to connect with audiences of all ages. His second book, *I Am My Brother's Keeper*, challenges men and families to embrace biblical brotherhood, accountability, and purpose in everyday life. Whether through preaching, writing, or teaching, Tony is committed to transforming hearts, strengthening homes, and advancing the Kingdom of God by empowering people to live authentically and intentionally.

His writings provide more than inspiration—they offer biblical truth, life application, and encouragement for men and families to live authentically, heal from silent struggles, and walk on purpose. Tony's leadership extends beyond the pulpit. His vision includes mentoring, teaching, and creating resources that strengthen the heart, the home, and the community. His long-term goal is to see his brand expand through books, speaking engagements, workshops, media features, and mentorship initiatives that create lasting impact.

At the core of his mission is transformation: moving people from confusion to clarity, isolation to connection, and survival to purpose. His life statement—"Faith over fear, calling over comfort, and purpose over position"—reflects his commitment to living what he teaches. Whether speaking to a congregation, mentoring one-on-one, or writing for a global audience, Tony Austin Jr. remains authentic, approachable, and purpose-driven, helping people become stronger in identity, deeper in faith, and fully committed to walking in the calling God has placed on their lives.

www.ingramcontent.com/pod-product-compliance
Lightning Source LLC
Chambersburg PA
CBHW072049160426
43197CB00014B/2695